500 FACTS

Space

www.pegasusforkids.com

© **B. Jain Publishers (P) Ltd.** All rights reserved. No part of this book may be reproduced, stored in a retrieval system or transmitted, in any form or by any means, mechanical, photocopying, recording or otherwise, without any prior written permission of the publisher.

Published by Kuldeep Jain for B. Jain Publishers (P) Ltd., D-157, Sector 63, Noida - 201307, U.P. Registered office: 1921/10, Chuna Mandi, Paharganj, New Delhi-110055

Printed in India

Preface 5

SPACE AND UNIVERSE

The Universe 6

GALAXIES IN SPACE

Galaxies 16

STARS

Life Cycle 34
Constellations 44

SOLAR SYSTEM

Sun 55
Mercury 70
Venus 75
Earth 81

Moon 99
Mars 109
Jupiter 113
Saturn 117
Uranus 121
Neptune 125
Pluto 129
Asteroids 133
Comets 136
Meteors 140

ASTRONOMY

Study of Astronomy 143
Telescopes 151
Satellites 158
Rockets 162
Humans in Space 170
Space Probes 177
Space Stations 184

PREFACE

Here is a fact, folks. There is no end to studying the infinite frontier that is space. The exploration of what goes on beyond our planet is the most incredible and epic journey humankind has ever undertaken.

The more you read and know about Space and the Universe, the more there is to know and find out. But why read and explore the space?

The exploration of space is directly related to Earth's past, present and future in relation to the Universe. Information about space allows us to know how we came to exist, what is our place in the Universe and many such fascinating aspects about the reality of the millions and millions of explored and unexplored aspects that are part of the Universe.

500 Facts on Space attempts to trace this never-ending journey of humanity in a fast-facts format. This book aims to inform you about whatever we know so far, and the possibilities that the future holds.

We not only aim to enhance your understanding of space and the Universe, but also hope that these facts will help add value to your knowledge of many things around you.

Happy Reading, Kids!

SPACE AND UNIVERSE

The Universe

1 The Universe is a vast expanse that covers everything that exists—from the Earth, Sun, stars and galaxies, to matter and energy. But did you know that it even includes time? Before Universe there was nothing, not even time, space or matter. In other words, the Universe that we know came from nothing and it was the origin of time!

2 How big is the Universe? The truth is that no one actually knows how big it is because the Universe is constantly expanding. But to give you an idea, just consider this—if you could somehow travel at the speed of light (300,000 km/sec), it would still take you about 100,000 years to cross the Milky Way!

3 **From the Earth it may seem as if the sky is full of stars, but in reality, the Universe is far less crowded.** Most of it is full of dark energy and dark matter—things that we cannot see. In fact, it is believed that if you collected all the stars, it would barely amount to half per cent of the Universe.

4 How old is our Universe? Scientists think that it is approximately 13.8 billion years old (keep in mind that it could be 130 million less or more). Our Solar System, including the Earth, is much younger, at 4.6 billion years old. This is about a third of the age of the Universe.

SPACE AND UNIVERSE

5 **The Universe is still a mysterious place and we are still learning new things about it every day.** The ancient Greek and Indian philosophers were the first to come up with a model of the Universe. This was the geocentric model. According to it, the Earth was the centre of the Universe, around which Sun, moon and planets revolved.

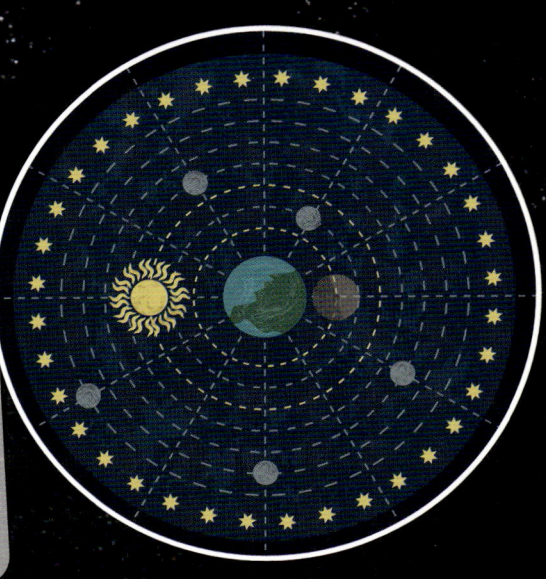

6 **After the geocentric model came the heliocentric model which was suggested by the Greeks.** According to this model, the Earth and other planets revolved around the Sun. This model was also adopted by some thinkers in medieval Europe, India and the Islamic world. However, at that time, it was not very widely accepted.

7 **The first philosopher who created mass acceptance of the heliocentric model was the 16th century astronomer Nicolaus Copernicus.** Since he was also a mathematician, Copernicus gave a geometric model, explaining in mathematical terms how the planets and the Sun move. Interestingly, this model was not perfect. However, it brought wider awareness about the heliocentric model.

THE UNIVERSE

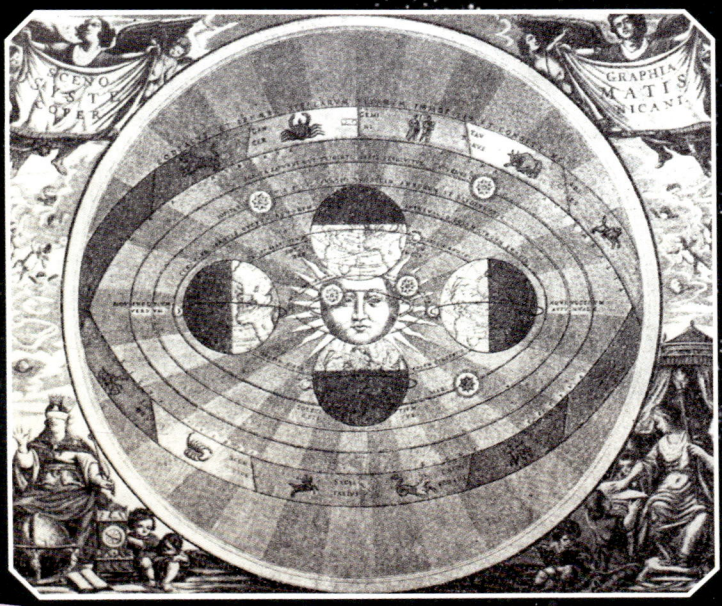

8 The Copernicus model established the idea that the Earth was not the centre of the Universe. Instead it revolved around the Sun. This idea later influenced many scientists including Isaac Newton. However, during Copernicus' lifetime it created an uproar in Europe because it was seen to be contrary to the Bible's teachings.

9 Copernicus' theory may have been banned, but it was later accepted by many great scientists like Galileo, Kepler and Isaac Newton, who helped us understand the Earth, Sun and stars much better. Slowly, people realised that even the heliocentric model was not correct—scientists found that the Sun was just one among many other stars in the Universe.

SPACE AND UNIVERSE

10 **Even as recently as 1920 we did not know how vast the Universe was and that the Solar System was just one among many other galaxies.** Scientists also discovered something even more interesting: these distant galaxies are actually moving away from us! Not just that, the speed of the movement is also slowly increasing.

11 Edwin Hubble, an American astronomer, first calculated how fast galaxies were moving. He discovered an interesting fact — the farther away a galaxy, the faster it is moving away from us. In fact, the Universe is not the same as it was yesterday and it is changing even as you read this!

THE UNIVERSE

12 In 1927, a Belgian physicist and priest, Georges Lemaître came up with a reason for the movement of galaxies. He suggested that these galaxies were moving because the Universe itself was expanding. In fact, he went a step further. If the Universe was growing bigger, it meant that it was once very small—like an atom. This was the basis of the Big Bang theory.

13 Not everyone agreed that the Universe started from a single point. In the mid-1920s, Fred Hoyle proposed the 'Steady State' model. According to him, the Universe had more or less remained the same, was only expanding as new matter was added to it. Interestingly, it was also Hoyle who came up with the term 'Big Bang' in a radio interview!

14 The Big Bang theory said that the Universe is expanding, and it is growing bigger every day. That means it must have been as small as tiny dense ball at the very beginning. The supporters of this theory claimed that there must have been a 'big bang' when that little ball of matter and energy exploded and formed our Universe.

SPACE AND UNIVERSE

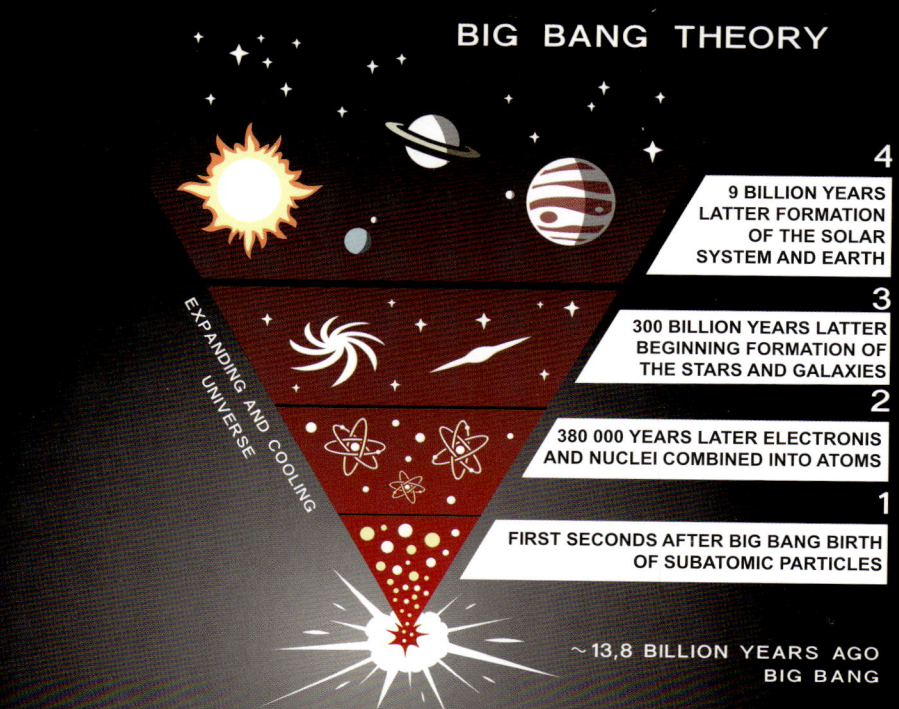

15 **In the 1940s, two scientists, Ralph Alpher and Robert Herman, reasoned that just after the Big Bang, the Universe must have been a hot and dense space.** As it cooled down, electrons and protons combined and photons were created. This resulted in radiation that should be present even today. They called this radiation the 'Cosmic Microwave Background' or CMB.

16 **In 1963, Arno Penzias and Robert Wilson decided to test the theory of CMB.** They reasoned that if present, CMB should be detectable with their Dicke radiometer. Unfortunately, there was too much disturbance. Thinking that it must be because of pigeon droppings on their antenna, the duo cleaned it up. However, the noise was still present. Eventually they realised that this disturbance was actually CMB!

THE UNIVERSE

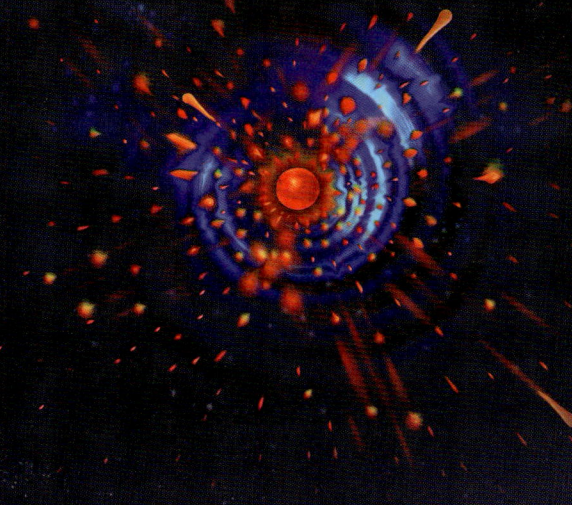

17 The discovery of CMB was important because it was taken as proof of the Big Bang, and of the universe expanding. CMB is like the fossil footprints of the Big Bang. Here's an interesting fact- it is everywhere around us. In other words, the echoes of the Big Bang, our origin, surrounds us everywhere!

18 Did you know that scientists actually have a name for the dense ball of energy that was the origin of the Universe? They call it the Singularity. Can you imagine that this huge Universe and everything in it was once squeezed into an unbelievably tiny point?

SPACE AND UNIVERSE

19 **The Singularity would have been a very hot, dense point.** Then in an instant, in about 10/34th of a second (that comes to about 10,000,000,000,000,000,000,000,000th of a second!) this singularity expanded in a sudden dramatic expansion at an incredible speed, faster than the speed of light. So, this singularity expanded to more than 90 times its size in a fraction of a second.

20 **As the Universe kept expanding, it started to cool down.** Scientists believe that in the first three minutes of its creation, the cosmos was made up of protons, electrons and neutrons. These were the building blocks of atoms that would later make everything we see, including our own bodies!

THE UNIVERSE

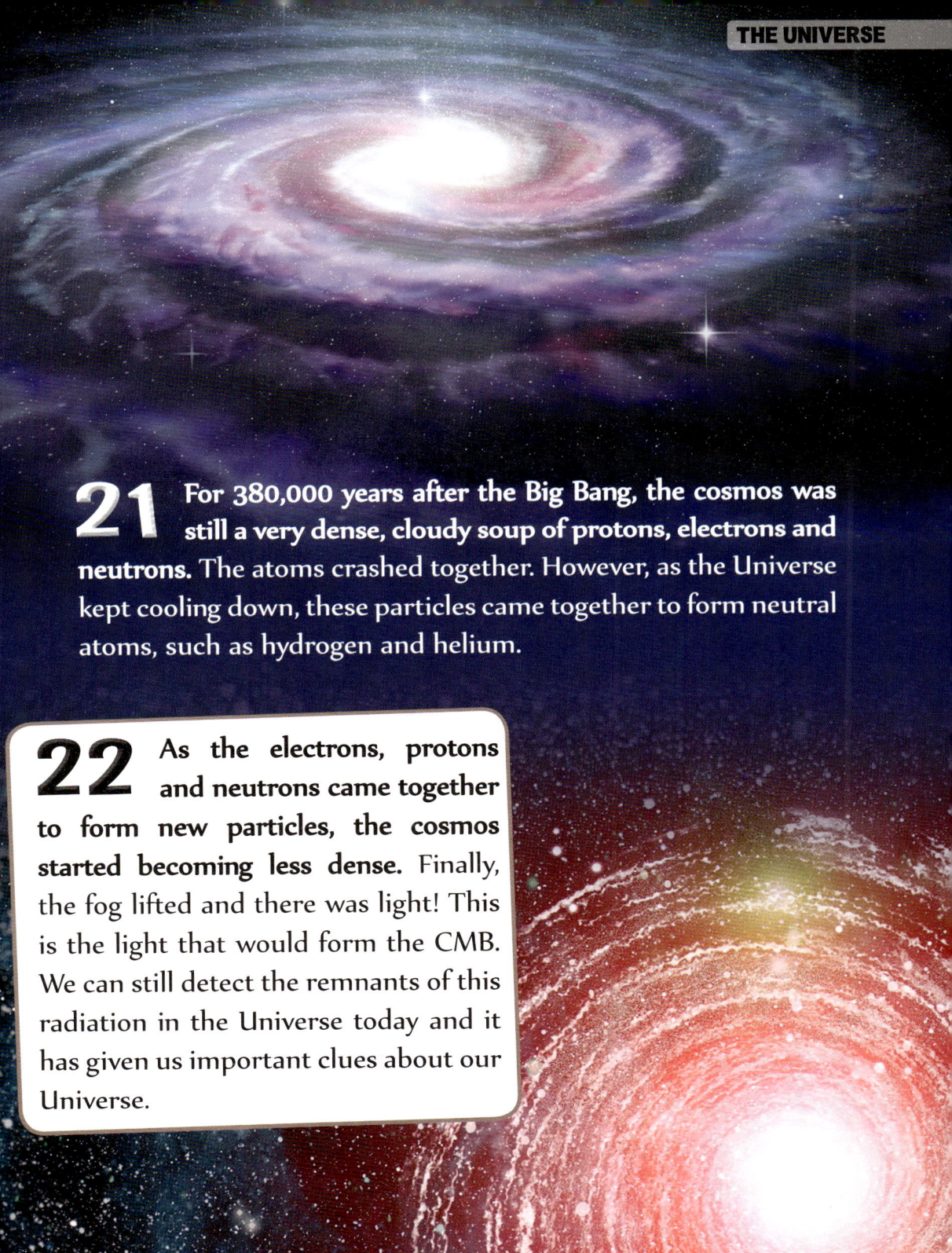

21 For 380,000 years after the Big Bang, the cosmos was still a very dense, cloudy soup of protons, electrons and neutrons. The atoms crashed together. However, as the Universe kept cooling down, these particles came together to form neutral atoms, such as hydrogen and helium.

22 As the electrons, protons and neutrons came together to form new particles, the cosmos started becoming less dense. Finally, the fog lifted and there was light! This is the light that would form the CMB. We can still detect the remnants of this radiation in the Universe today and it has given us important clues about our Universe.

GALAXIES IN SPACE

Galaxies

23 **Despite the light that finally appeared, the Universe was still a very dark space.** This is because gases such as hydrogen present in the Universe absorbed the light. After approximately 400 million years, as the Universe cooled further, the hydrogen condensed. With the hydrogen clearing up, the so called 'dark age' lifted.

24 **We still know very little about the Universe or how it was formed.** What we do know is mostly through observation, calculations and then interpretation of the results. Scientists are constantly studying distant stars and galaxies to find out more about the birth of the Universe. Ultimately, the birth of the Universe is also the story of our origin.

25 Galaxies are vast space systems of stars, dust, gas, dark matter and star clusters. The word 'galaxy' comes from the Greek word *galaxies* which means 'milky'. It refers to our own galaxy, the Milky Way. The word was used because our galaxy appears as a foggy or milky band of light.

26 Galaxies are really vast. Even the smaller galaxies, known as 'dwarfs', have at least at least 10 million stars. The bigger galaxies, known as 'giants', have 100 trillion stars! The sun is just one among the 100 million stars in the Milky Way. Scientists estimate that there could be more than 200 galaxies in the Universe!

GALAXIES IN SPACE

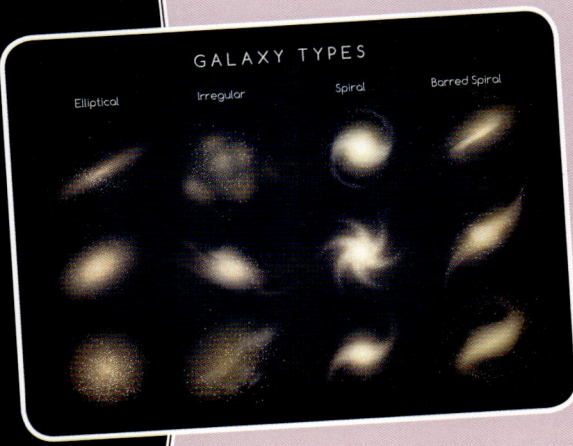

27 **Galaxies do not just come in different sizes, they also come in different shapes.** Galaxies are divided into four types according to their shape: spiral, elliptical, barred spiral and irregular. Spiral galaxies have arms that spiral around a centre, barred spiral have a bar at the core, elliptical are elliptical-shaped. Other shapes are lumped under 'irregular' galaxies.

28 **Galaxies are of different shapes because of gravity.** Most galaxies have a heavy centre of gravity around which makes the stars move in a specific pattern. This movement, which is usually spiral or elliptical, decides the galaxy's shape. Irregular galaxies can appear asymmetrical because they are under the gravitational effect of another nearby galaxy.

GALAXIES

29 **At the centre of most massive galaxies lies a supermassive Black Hole.** They are named so because they are huge in size with a mass that can be equal to a billion suns! Scientists believe that these Black Holes play an important role in the galaxy, influencing its size and the orbits of surrounding stars.

30 **Where did these galaxies come from? Some believe that the Universe and these galaxies have existed in this manner at all times.** However, recent scientific discoveries have shown us that galaxies were born over time. Also, scientists believe that galaxies are not very stable structures. Galaxies are always changing and moving in space.

GALAXIES IN SPACE

31 The formation of galaxies took place a long time after the Big Bang, the event that gave birth to the Universe. As with all other parts of the Universe, the building blocks of stars were also the protons, electrons and neutrons. These stars would form the galaxies later on.

32 Galaxies were formed during the 'dark ages' of the Universe. This was a little after the Universe was born. The protons, electrons and neutrons had cooled down to form hydrogen and helium. These gases absorbed light to create a dark dense space. However, these gases also reacted with other matter to form massive cold cloudy structures, which would later form galaxies.

GALAXIES

33 **How did the stars appear?** Over a long period of time, the cloudy Universe continued to expand. All the energy and matter that was moving through space kept colliding. From these collisions, new elements were formed. In the process, heat and light were released. This light became visible once the gases floating in space cooled down and re-combined. It was now that the first stars appeared.

34 **One of the most important components that went into making galaxies is gravity.** The stars that first appeared slowly moved closer, forming galaxies. Later, planets also formed around some of these stars, like our own Solar System. Interestingly, gravity also influenced the stars' movement and a galaxy's shape.

GALAXIES IN SPACE

35 **Did you know that galaxies often cross paths?** As a galaxy moves around in the Universe, it can often run across another galaxy. The results of these mergers are often quite dramatic. In such situations, we can get the most stunning visuals of celestial clashes. Mergers can also change the very character of galaxies, creating new stars and orbits.

36 **Stars rarely ever collide during a merger.** There is usually enough empty space in galaxies for stars to cross without colliding. However, a merger can have other more lasting effects. As the galaxies come closer, the gravitational forces within each galaxy cause the stars to change their orbits in a highly erratic fashion. As a result, merged galaxies often change shapes.

GALAXIES

37 A significant impact of galaxy mergers is new star formation. While stars almost never collide during a merger, gases and molecular matter clash with some dramatic reactions. One of these is the formation of new stars. In fact, galaxy mergers are a rich ground for the birth of new stars.

38 Scientists believe that many elliptical galaxies are actually the result of galaxy mergers. The random orbit of stars of elliptical galaxies and their structure suggest that these are the result of mergers. Some of the largest galaxies in the Universe are elliptical and these are often found among galaxy clusters.

GALAXIES IN SPACE

39 Did you know that sometimes a galaxy may 'cannibalise' another? This happens when a giant galaxy collides with a much smaller one. While the larger galaxy remains relatively unchanged, the smaller one is usually ripped apart. In fact, the Milky Way is believed to be cannibalising smaller galaxies like the Sagittarius Dwarf and the Canis Major Dwarf galaxies.

40 Scientists try to study such galaxy mergers to find important clues about how galaxies are evolving. Mergers are fertile ground for star formation, orbit change and to learn more about galaxy behaviour. These are seen as violent behaviour because they can end up enlarging a galaxy, ripping apart a small galaxy and creating new celestial bodies.

GALAXIES

41 For us, the most important galaxy is, of course, the Milky Way because this is where we are located in the vast Universe. The name 'Milky Way' comes from the Greek words for 'milk circle'. The name was chosen because from the Earth the Milky Way has a disk-like milky white appearance.

42 **The Milky Way is a barred spiral galaxy. It has a bulging centre, which appears like a bar with four spiralling arms.** There are actually two major arms, two minor arms and a couple of smaller spurs. The Solar System falls in one of these smaller spurs, between two major arms.

GALAXIES IN SPACE

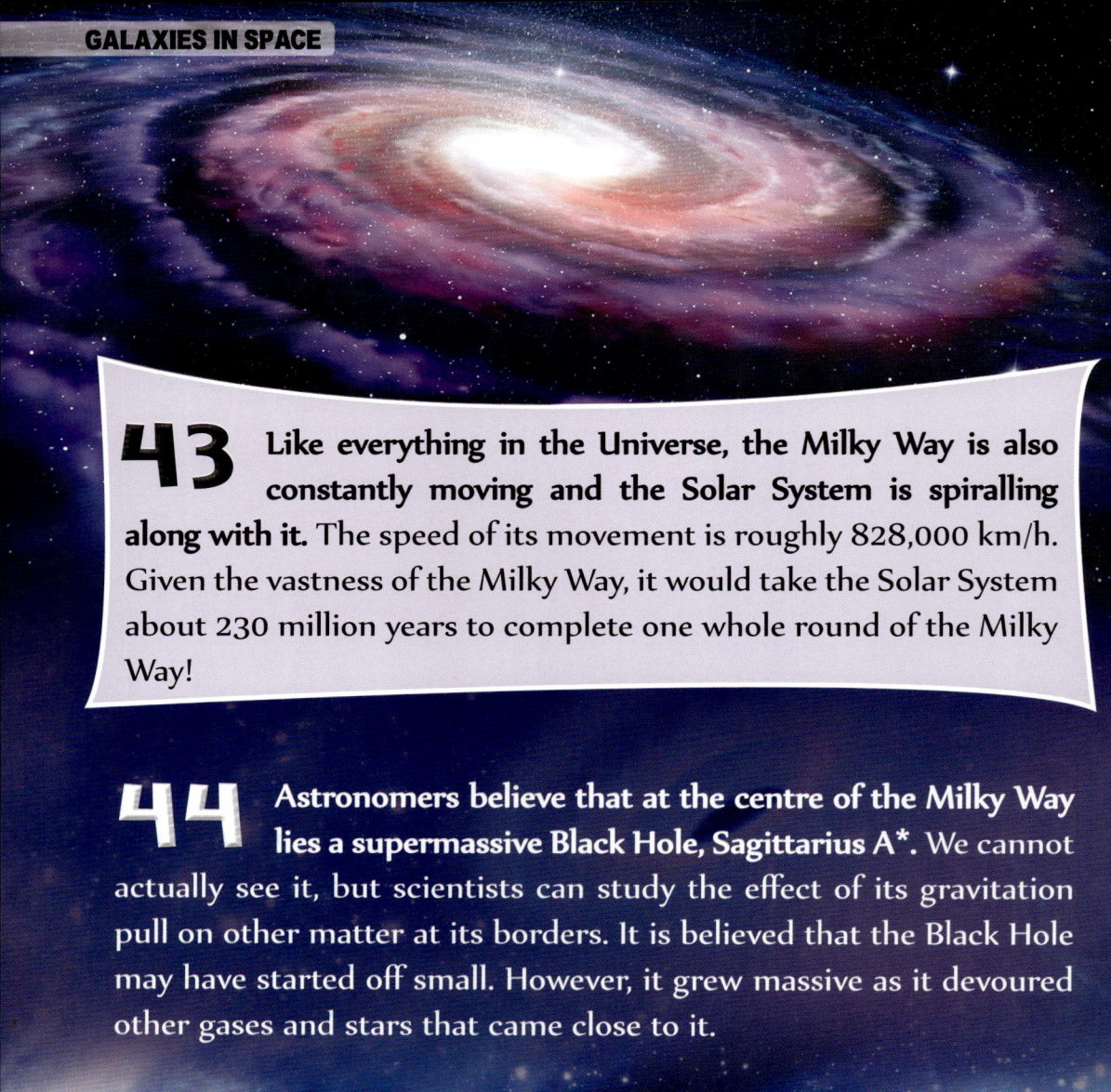

43 **Like everything in the Universe, the Milky Way is also constantly moving and the Solar System is spiralling along with it.** The speed of its movement is roughly 828,000 km/h. Given the vastness of the Milky Way, it would take the Solar System about 230 million years to complete one whole round of the Milky Way!

44 **Astronomers believe that at the centre of the Milky Way lies a supermassive Black Hole, Sagittarius A*.** We cannot actually see it, but scientists can study the effect of its gravitation pull on other matter at its borders. It is believed that the Black Hole may have started off small. However, it grew massive as it devoured other gases and stars that came close to it.

45 The Milky Way may seem like it is lit up with stars, but most of it is just dark matter. In fact, dark matter accounts for 90 per cent of its mass. Like Black Holes, scientists cannot see dark matter. However its effect can be seen in the behaviour of the galaxy and the speed of its movement. It also gives our galaxy a 'halo' effect.

46 The Milky Way is believed to be almost as old as the Universe itself. It would have been formed shortly after the Big Bang as gases and molecular matter condensed to form stars. We can estimate its age by calculating the age of the oldest stars in the galaxy and studying how they were formed.

GALAXIES IN SPACE

47 **The Milky Way looks like it is surrounded by a halo.** This halo is not the one you imagine around Gods and angels. In fact, it is invisible to the naked eye. The halo is made of stellar material, globular clusters and gases. This halo extends to thousands of light years, touching nearby galaxies.

48 **The Milky Way did not always look the way we see it today.** In fact, it was a small dense cloud that later expanded and formed into a galaxy. At first, it was a much smaller galaxy. However, over millions of years it has grown, gobbling up smaller galaxies to become the giant it is today.

GALAXIES

49 **The Sun is among the 200 billion stars that make the Milky Way.** Most of these stars are much older than the Sun, which is just 4.5-billion-year-old. Many of the stars are now red dwarfs (a star that has cooled down and become smaller). Scientists estimate that the Sun is roughly 30,000 light years away from the centre of the Universe.

50 **The Milky Way may seem immense, but it is just a very small part of the Universe.** As we go farther away, we will find that Milky Way is part of a large cluster of galaxies. Along with 50 other galaxies, it is part of the 'Local Group'. Farther out, it is part of an even bigger cluster known as the 'Virgo Supercluster'.

GALAXIES IN SPACE

51 Scientists are not very sure about the total number of galaxies in the Local Group. This is because new galaxies are still being discovered, and smaller ones may merge with larger ones. Some of these galaxies are so faint or small that they are not easily detected by astronomers.

52 The Local Group of galaxies has a gravitational centre. It lies between the Andromeda galaxy and the Milky Way—the two largest galaxies of the cluster. This means that the galaxies within the group are gravitationally bound to each other. While other galaxies may be moving away from each other, the galaxies in the group are most likely moving closer.

GALAXIES

53 The three biggest galaxies in the Local Group in order of size are: the Andromeda galaxy, Milky Way and Triangulum galaxy. Our closest neighbouring galaxies are Sagittarius Dwarf Elliptical Galaxy and Canis Major Dwarf Galaxy. Both will soon become a part of the Milky Way as it 'cannibalises' them. A little farther away are the Large and Small Magellanic Clouds.

54 Like the Milky Way, Andromeda is also a spiral galaxy. It is 2.5 million light years away from Earth. Astronomers estimate that it has roughly one trillion stars, twice that of the Milky Way. Again, like the Milky Way, it also has a number of satellite galaxies and globular clusters.

GALAXIES IN SPACE

55 **Did you know that we can actually see the Andromeda Galaxy from Earth with the naked eye?** At a size of 220,000 light years across, it is the largest galaxy in the Local Group. Coupled with its closeness to Earth and its brightness (with one trillion stars), it can be seen clearly from Earth without the aid of any magnifying devise like a telescope.

56 **Astronomers have deduced that Andromeda and the Milky Way are likely to collide in the future!** We don't need to panic yet, though. This fairly spectacular event won't happen for at least the next 3.75 billion years. The Sun would have become a red dwarf by then, ending life on Earth as we know it.

GALAXIES

57 **The third largest galaxy in the Local Group is the Triangulum Galaxy.** Some astronomers believe that it could be a satellite of the Andromeda Galaxy. On a clear night, we can see it with the naked eye as a distant object in the night sky. Like Andromeda and Milky Way, it is also a spiral galaxy.

58 **Our neighbouring galaxies have or will have a profound impact on our own.** Studying their behaviour provides astronomers with important clues on galaxy evolution and gives an insight into the history and future of our own Milky Way. This in turn gives us a better understanding of the origin of the Universe.

STARS

Life Cycle

59 **Stars are glowing, spherical objects, full of matter called plasma.** Plasma is the fourth state of matter after solid, liquid and gas. All stars are made of two gases—hydrogen and helium. The hydrogen accounts for 75%, while the helium makes up 25% of the matter of a star. As a star ages, hydrogen slowly converts to helium. Thus, an old star will have greater amounts of helium.

60 **Stars have always prompted our curiosity.** Our forefathers thought that stars were divine. They used stars to predict the future. Stars were also used by navigators to pinpoint their location. The study of stars was closely linked to religion, later developing into a science known as astronomy. Even today, the study of stars gives us important clues about the Universe.

LIFE CYCLE

61 **There are countless stars in the Universe, more than there are grains of sand on all the beaches on Earth.** The Milky Way alone has 200 to 400 billion stars and astronomers think that there could be more than 500 billion such galaxies! Remember, this number is not static, because new stars are born quite frequently.

62 **Although stars are mostly just composed of hydrogen and helium, they are the eventual source of other heavy metals in the Universe, like oxygen, carbon and nitrogen.** The composition of a star determines the composition of its revolving planetary system and the atmosphere of each planet.

STARS

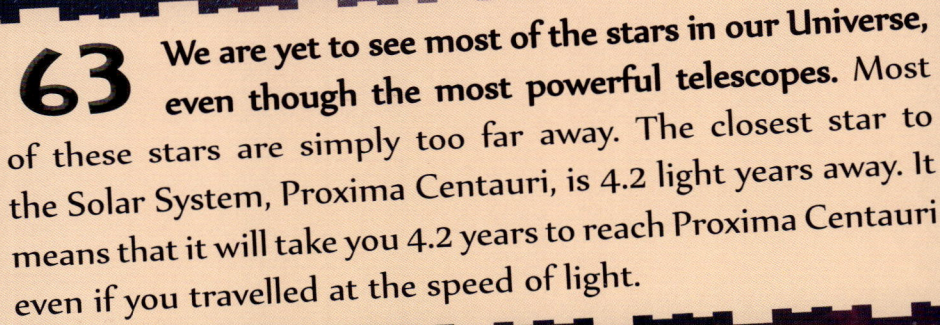

63 We are yet to see most of the stars in our Universe, even though the most powerful telescopes. Most of these stars are simply too far away. The closest star to the Solar System, Proxima Centauri, is 4.2 light years away. It means that it will take you 4.2 years to reach Proxima Centauri even if you travelled at the speed of light.

64 Like many living things, stars also take birth, age and then die. Stars are born out of dense clouds of gas known as molecular clouds. These areas are also known as stellar nurseries. Such areas of dense clouds of gas, dust and stellar remains can be found in many parts of the Universe.

LIFE CYCLE

65 The molecular clouds that form the stars are made of hydrogen and helium with a few trace elements. The hydrogen accounts for almost 70 per cent of the cloud, the helium amounts to 23 to 28 per cent and the rest is made up by heavy metals, usually left over from other stars as they pass through their lifecycle.

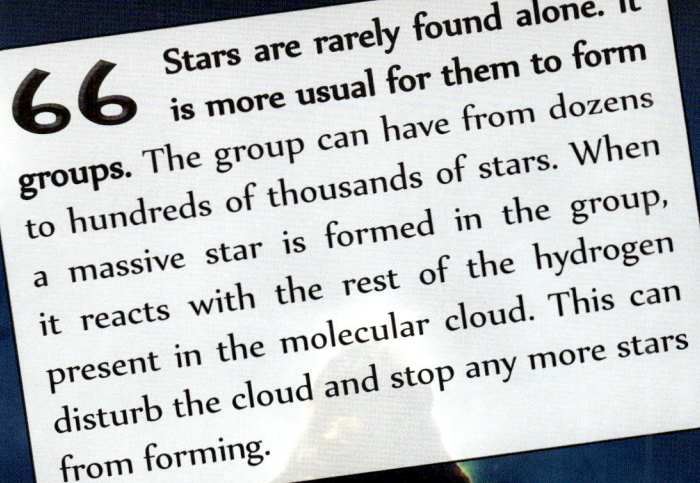

66 Stars are rarely found alone. It is more usual for them to form groups. The group can have from dozens to hundreds of thousands of stars. When a massive star is formed in the group, it reacts with the rest of the hydrogen present in the molecular cloud. This can disturb the cloud and stop any more stars from forming.

67 Stars are formed when a big mass of molecular cloud forms its own gravitational pull and starts to break up. The gravitational energy of each of these parts is released as heat. As a result, both the pressure and the temperature build up and the broken fragment is transformed into a rotating spherical ball. This is the proto-star.

68 The proto-star is a super-hot, dense spherical ball. Its temperature continues to rise due to its motion. At the same time, it also reacts with the surrounding gas to grow bigger. As the core temperature and pressure reaches 1 million degree Celsius, the atomic nuclei start to fuse and an incredible amount of energy is released, igniting the star!

69 Not all the surrounding gas and dust become part of a star. Some of the matter turns into planets, asteroid or comets. Some of it may remain as dust scattered near a star. The gravitational force of a star will force the matter to remain within the same space and not float away. In fact, it is gravity that creates stars and keeps planets and asteroids in orbit around them.

70 Astronomers categorise stars according to their mass— Intermediate-mass stars, High-mass stars and Low-mass stars. A star will spend most of its life as a main sequence star, but as it grows older, its fate will depend on its mass. A star's mass also affects its glow and the effect on its surrounding.

71 **The Sun is an Intermediate-mass star.** Any star that falls between eight times to half the Sun's mass falls in this category. High-mass stars are more than eight times the mass of the Sun, and Low-mass stars have less than half to a tenth of the Sun's mass. Objects with even lesser mass usually become failed stars.

72 **A star spends its life trying to maintain balance.** On one hand, it is affected by the core gravitational force of its own mass, that keeps pulling it inwards. To stop it from complete collapse, there is an opposing force within the star—nuclear energy. The nuclear energy produced in the core counters the gravitational force and creates a balance.

LIFE CYCLE

73 **The creation of a 'death star' is linked to the loss of this balance.** After all the hydrogen in the core is used up, the energy dispelled by the nuclear fusion also ends. Gravity becomes the dominating force, squashing all the matter into the core, heating it up. What happens after that depends on the mass of the star.

74 **In Intermediate stars, once the hydrogen in the core is exhausted the fusion now shifts towards the outer layers.** Thus, the outer disk is pushed away as it cools down and becomes a red giant. The helium core increases in size and temperature, leading to an explosive helium flash. The radius of the star contracts, but its temperature goes up.

75 **Massive stars become Red Super Giants after expansion. Fusion continues even after the helium is used up.** Heavier elements go through fusion, beginning with carbon, followed by neon, oxygen and silicon. Fusion takes place in concentric rings around the core. The final stage comes when iron is produced at the core.

STARS

76 **Sometimes gravity can create a Supernova.** When gravity shrinks the core of a star to a much smaller size, it can rebound. This causes fusion in the outer layers. The star then explodes in a Supernova. Smaller stars become Neutron stars with a neutron core. More massive stars find their gravitational pull too strong and collapse to form a Black Hole.

77 **The gravitational force of a black hole is so strong that even light cannot escape it.** This is why they appear to be completely black! In fact, we were unaware of Black Holes till X-Ray astronomy was invented! Astronomers study Black Holes with the help of satellites and telescopes that are travelling through space.

78 **A Black Hole has a dramatic impact on the space around it.** In fact, this is how we know there is a Black Hole in the vicinity! Black Holes warp or bend time and space in its immediate perimeter. As a result, stars and gas can be found orbiting around it. Stars often emit high energy light that scientists can detect. By observing the warping of these emissions, they can identify nearby Black Holes.

79 **We know that a galaxy is made up of billions of stars.** However we still do not know how many stars there are, exactly. To find the exact figure we need to know the exact mass of the galaxy and how much of that is made up of stars. Unfortunately, we cannot even guess either of these factors with any certainty.

80 **The most important star for us is the Sun. It has a radius of 695,508 kms.** It is equal to 332,946 times the mass of the Earth. Roughly 73 per cent of this mass is hydrogen, 25 per cent is helium, and the rest is made of heavier elements. It is now fairly middle-aged. It is believed that in about five billion years it will become a Red Giant.

Constellations

81 Stars are rarely ever lonely like the Sun. Stars are formed in dense molecular clouds and this often results in two or more stars being formed close together. This is why we often find that many stars appear together. Sometimes these stars appear together in a pattern. They are called constellations.

82 Stars of a constellation may appear closely placed in the sky, but in reality, these are many light years apart. They only appear close from our point of view on the Earth. Their position also changes according to the Earth's path on its orbit. This is why our forefathers used them to keep track of the changing seasons.

83 The word 'constellation' comes from the Latin word 'cōnstellātiō', which means 'set of stars'. Their position in the sky was used to map directions and predict seasons. Many of our forefathers saw constellations as heavenly beings with magic powers. Many civilisations also used them to predict the future!

CONSTELLATIONS

84 **Our fascination with constellations date back centuries.** The first record of constellations being identified dates back to 17,000 years ago, in southern France, where the Lascaux cave paintings appear to depict the Pleiades and Hyades clusters. A more detailed account appears in Mesopotamian tablets from 1300 to 1000 BC.

85 **Most of the constellations are named after myths and legends of the ancient Greek and Roman civilisations.** They, in turn, followed the ancient Babylonians, who were the first to mathematically chart constellations. The history of astronomy in India dates back to the Indus Valley civilisation. In fact, constellations as part of astrology also appear in the Vedic literature.

STARS

86 Did you know that the Greek astronomer and mathematician Claudius Ptolemy identified and named as many as 48 constellations that are followed even today? Although the definition of constellation may have changed, Ptolemy's nomenclature still stands. In his book, *Almagest*, he presented a geometric model based on observations that dated back to 800 years!

87 Many of the star groupings we think are constellations are actually not. Whereas the ancient civilisations saw constellations as patterns made by stars, in modern astronomy constellations are defined as rectangular divisions of the sky that include all the stars that fall within the area. It helps astronomers to classify new stars.

88 There are 88 modern constellations. These include 48 classical constellations by the Greeks as well as 12 zodiac signs. However, in modern astronomy constellations include a much wider boundary. For example, the constellation of Ursa Major includes the larger group of stars around it as well.

CONSTELLATIONS

89 An asterism is a group of stars that do not form an official constellation, but are recognised by the lay person as such. For example, the Big Dipper is popularly known as a constellation but it is actually an asterism. It is part of the larger Ursa Major constellation. Asterism thus refers to patterns, whereas constellations refer to an area in the sky.

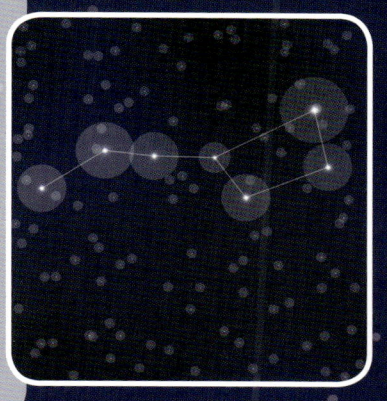

90 You cannot see every constellation from one point on Earth. The visibility is not just affected by your position, but also by seasons. As the Earth revolves around the Sun, different parts of the Universe are visible to us at different times of the year. Constellations are divided into two groups: the Northern Constellations that appear in the Northern hemisphere and Southern Constellations that appear in the Southern hemisphere.

91 Some of the most familiar constellations are the zodiac signs. Many ancient civilisations believed that the 12 constellations that form the zodiac signs were divine and their positions in the sky to predict the future. These were based on the Sun, moon and a planet's orbit through the sky.

STARS

92 The zodiac signs are not actually constellations. Although modern astronomy follows ancient names, the zodiacs do not always fall in the constellation area that is named after it. The 12 zodiac signs are Aries, Taurus, Gemini, Cancer, Leo, Virgo, Libra, Scorpio, Sagittarius, Capricorn, Aquarius and Pisces.

93 The largest constellation is Hydra, which covers an area of 1303 square degrees. Measuring over 100 degrees, it is the longest constellation. It also appears in the 48 classical Greek constellations. With a long twisting shape, it was known as 'the snake' in mythology. It has 17 primary stars and 75 Bayer/Flamsteed designation stars.

94 The closest galaxy to the Milky Way, Andromeda, appears in the Andromeda constellation. It is part of the Northern Constellations. Andromeda is the 19th largest constellation. It also dates back to the classical Greek constellations. It is named after Princess Andromeda, wife of Perseus in Greek mythology.

CONSTELLATIONS

95 One of the constellations that can be seen across the earth is Orion. Its wide visibility is due to its position on the Celestial equator (corresponding to Earth's equator). It is named after the mythical Greek hunter, Orion. The asterism has seven bright stars that make an hourglass pattern, which is said to look like the body of a man.

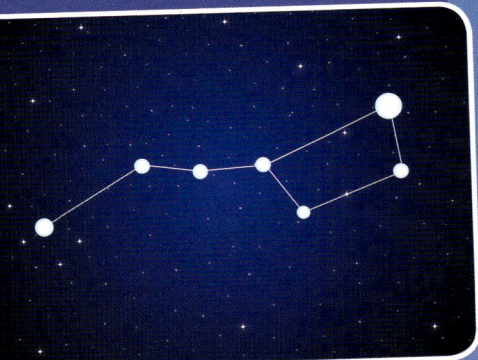

96 The constellation of Ursa Major appears in famous works of fiction as well as in the Bible! The name 'Ursa Major' is Latin for 'great she-bear'. Hence, it is also known as the Great Bear. As we already know, the asterism Big Dipper is a part of the Ursa Major constellation. Apart from its mythological importance, it was also used as a navigational tool for centuries.

97 Corresponding to Ursa Major is the constellation of Ursa Minor, which means 'little bear' in Latin. It includes a seven-star asterism known as the Little Dipper, similar to the Big Dipper. It contains Polaris, also known as the North Star. Since Polaris is located above the northern celestial pole (corresponding to the North Pole), it also serves as an important navigational tool.

STARS

98 **Appearing in the Northern sky, Pegasus is the seventh-largest constellation in the sky.** It is named after the Greek mythical winged horse, Pegasus. It contains a square-shaped asterism—the Pegasus. One of the stars from the asterism, Pegasus actually falls in the neighbouring constellation of Andromeda.

Canis Major

99 **An important constellation in the Southern sky is Canis Major.** It is Latin for 'greater dog'. It represents one of the four dogs following Orion, the hunter, in mythological stories. This asterism contains Sirius, the brightest star in the night sky. Its neighbouring constellation is Canis Minor, representing the 'smaller dog' following Orion.

100 **Another prominent constellation in the Northern sky is Cygnus.** The name comes from the Latin word for 'swan'. This is a cross-shaped asterism, which is why it is also known as the Northern Cross. It also contains the Hercules–Corona Borealis Great Wall, the biggest celestial structure in the observable Universe.

Cygnus
Swan

CONSTELLATIONS

101 **Aquarius is a well-known constellation. It is also one of the zodiac signs.** The constellation contains one of the oldest globular clusters in the Universe, the M2. It has roughly 100,000 stars, packed tightly into a dense ball. It is home to the star system Gliese 876, which contains one of the most Earth-like planets yet discovered!

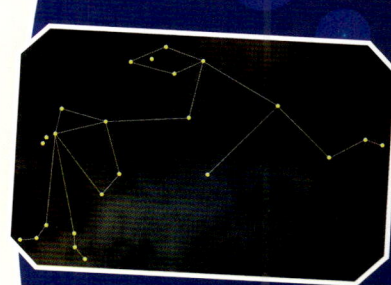

102 **The Aquila constellation appears over the equator.** Aquila is Latin for 'eagle'. The name came from the Greek legend of Zeus' eagle that carried his thunderbolts. The brightest star in this constellation is the Altair. It forms the 'head' of the eagle, while two other stars—Epsilon Aquilae and Zeta—form the 'tail'. These are stars actually multiple star systems.

103 **Aries is one the oldest known constellations, and is seen clearly from the Northern hemisphere.** Aries is Latin for 'ram', representing the golden ram in Greek mythology. It is a mid-sized constellation and is not very bright. The importance of this constellation lies in its location. In astronomy, when Aries appears in the night sky, it marks the beginning of spring in the Northern hemisphere.

STARS

104 One of the most easily visible constellations is the Cassiopeia. The name comes from Queen Cassiopeia from Greek mythology. It is one of the classical constellations named by Ptolemy. Its main asterism, Cassiopeia, has a distinct shape with five stars forming a 'W'. Cassiopeia is home to several bright, massive stars. Recently, two supernovae took place in this cluster.

GEMINI

105 To the left of Orion is the constellation Gemini. This word is Latin for 'twins' and represents Castor and Pollux, the twin brothers of Helen of Troy. The asterism Gemini contains two roughly parallel lines of stars. At the top of each line shines a bright star—Castor at the top of one, and Pollux over the other. Pollux is the brighter star, while Castor is actually a star system.

106 With a number of bright stars and a distinct asterism, Leo is a prominent constellation in the sky. Leo is Latin for 'lion', representing the Nemean Lion from Greek mythology. It actually contains two distinct patterns that together form the asterism that resembles a crouching lion. The constellation is home to many distinct celestial objects including many bright stars.

CONSTELLATIONS

107 One of the brightest constellations in the sky is Scorpius, Latin for scorpion. It is home to a number of bright stars, making it easily visible. The Scorpius is associated with Orion, the hunter of Greek mythology. Part of the Southern sky, it is one of the larger constellations.

108 Taurus is a large and prominent constellation in the Northern sky. Latin for 'bull', Taurus has a number of mythologies associated with it. Two open clusters—Hyades and Pleiades—that are visible from Earth form Taurus. The brightest star in the constellation is a Red Giant named Aldebaran. It also contains the Taurus-Auriga complex, a star formation region.

109 The smallest constellation—associated with the zodiac sign Capricorn—among the zodiac signs is the Capricornus, appearing in the Southern sky. In Latin, it means 'goat horn' or 'horned goat'. The main Asterism is formed by a triangle of bright stars, meant to represent the mythical goat. Although fairly faint, this constellation has always been part of astrological calculations.

STARS

110 In the Northern sky lies the Draco constellation. It is a circumpolar galaxy, which means that it never sets below the horizon. You can see it throughout the year in the Northern hemisphere. The name Draco is Latin for 'dragon'. Like many classical constellations, this name also comes from Greek mythology.

DRACO

111 The second largest constellation is Virgo. It is easy to spot because of the bright star Spica. You can find it by following the curve of the Big Dipper. It contains the first discovered extra-solar planetary system. Although it may seem rather void to the naked eye, Virgo is actually home to several galaxy clusters.

112 The meaning and significance of constellations may have changed, but they are equally important for astronomers today. By dividing the sky between these constellations, we have created a detailed map of the observable Universe. Like our forefathers, constellations are now an important part of our understanding of the Universe.

SOLAR SYSTEM

Sun

113 Around 5,000 million years back the Sun was formed from a cloud of gas and dust. The Sun is one of the oldest stars and a great source of heat, light and energy. It generates heat and light through a process called nuclear fusion. It is continuing to heat up with the passage of time. Scientists estimate that the Sun is becoming 10 per cent more luminous every billion years.

114 The Sun is a luminous ball of hot gases, mainly hydrogen (74 per cent) and helium (24 per cent). The remaining two per cent includes amounts of iron, nickel, oxygen and other elements present in our Solar System. Do you know the temperature inside the Sun is around 14,000,000 degree Celsius? The surface temperature of the Sun is about 5,500 degree Celsius, but at its centre it is about 15 million degree Celsius.

SOLAR SYSTEM

115 The outer surface of the Sun is made up of three main layers: the photosphere, the chromosphere, and the corona. Do you know that dark patches on the Sun's surface are sunspots caused due to magnetic fields? Spots have a dark central region called the umbra and lighter outer region called penumbra.

116 Solar flares and prominences are huge flames of hot gas that arise from sunspots. These solar flares can harm the Earth by damaging its ionosphere. Moreover, it can break radio signals and disturb satellites' orbits. Flares are very short-lived; just like bursts of light. However, a large prominence can last for months.

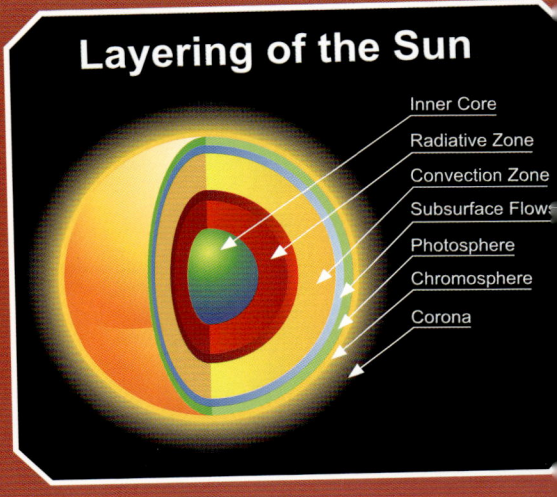

117 It is interesting to note that the Sun's diameter is 108 times greater than that of the Earth and its average radius is 695,508 kilometres. Do you know that the Sun generates its own solar winds? These winds occur when the magnetic field of the Sun extends into space.

118

The Sun actually contains 99.86 per cent of the total mass of the Solar System. Its mass is 330,000 times greater than that of the Earth. The Sun is almost spherical in the shape. Scientists have calculated that there is only a 10-kilometre difference between its polar and equatorial diameters. The Sun is also known as a yellow dwarf star.

119

Do you know that the distance between the Sun and Earth keeps changing through the year? The distance between the Earth and the Sun is called an Astronomical Unit (AU). The Sun is not stationary; it is travelling through space at a speed of 220 kilometres per second.

120

The Sun has a strong magnetic field. It releases energy during magnetic storms which results in occurrence of solar flares and sunspots. During this time, magnetic lines twist and spin, just like tornados do on the Earth. Did you know that the Sun rotates quicker at its equator as compared to its poles? This is known as differential rotation.

121 The Sun is the source of light and heat for Earth. From prehistoric times, people have been worshipping the Sun. Many different cultures around the world referred to the Sun god, by different names. For instance, in ancient Egypt, the Sun god was called Ra.

122 The outer surface of the Sun, which is easily visible, is called the photosphere. It has a temperature of around 5000–6,000 degree Celsius. Beneath the outer layer of the Sun lies the convection zone, followed by the radiative zone where heat can only travel through radiation. At the centre of the Sun lies the core.

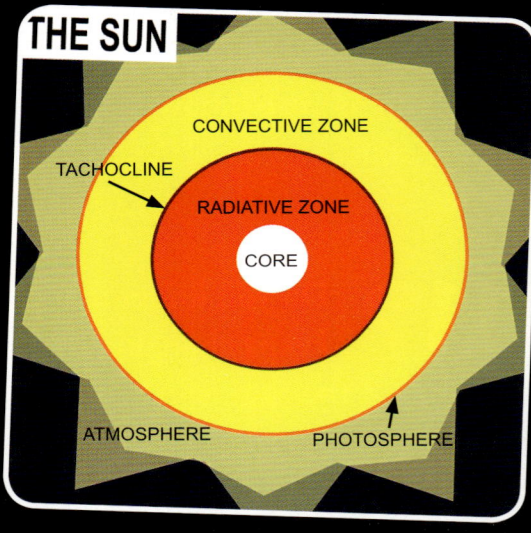

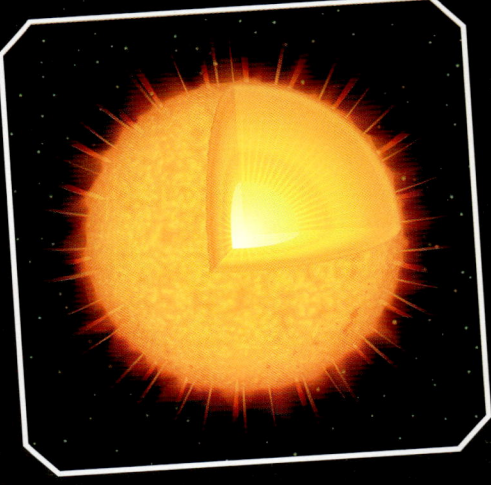

123 The Sun is a big sphere of hydrogen gas. As it keeps rotating, its different parts keep moving at different speed too. By keeping a record of movement of the sunspots across its surface, the speed of its rotation can be calculated. For instance, the area at the equator takes 25 days to finish one rotation, while at the poles it can take up to 36 days.

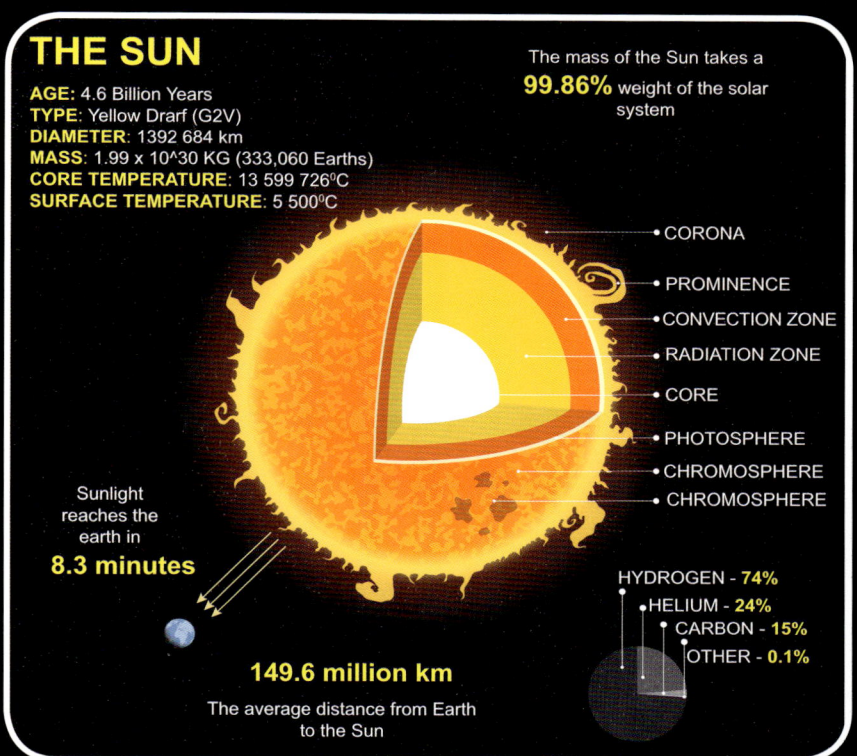

124 **Scientists have estimated that there is a difference in the temperature between the outer atmosphere and the surface of the Sun.** The surface can heat up to 6,000 degree Celsius, but its heating temperature is less than that of the Sun's atmosphere. At the chromosphere, the temperature can reach 100,000 degree Celsius. The corona can extend to a temperature even greater than the core of the Sun, sometimes reaching 1 million degree Celsius.

125 **Do you know that there are many space crafts which are constantly studying the Sun?** Of these, the most well-known is the Solar and Heliospheric Observatory (SOHO) made by NASA and the ESA. It was launched in December 1995. It is still in space and continues to send photographs and information about the Sun.

SOLAR SYSTEM

126 A more recent observatory is NASA's STEREO. Launched on October 2006, it is a twin space-based observatory. One observatory is ahead of Earth in its orbit, while the other trails behind it. The two together provide a 3-D perspective about the Sun's activity. This will help astronomers to study both the structure and evolution of solar storms as they blast from the Sun and move through space.

127 Do you know that the Sun is likely to one day consume the Earth? After 130 million years, the Sun will start burning hydrogen instead of helium. This will result in its expansion. It will convert into a Red Giant star and engulf Mercury, Venus and finally Earth.

128 What is the speed of the Sun? It moves at 220 kilometres per second. It takes 225–250 million years, approximately, to complete one orbit of the Milky Way galaxy. It is about 24,000-26,000 light years away from the galactic centre.

129 **Do you know how long light from the Sun takes to reach Earth?** The average distance from the Sun to the Earth is about 150 million kilometres. Light travels at 300,000 kilometres per second. Thus, it takes 500 seconds or eight minutes and twenty seconds for sunlight to reach the Earth. That is not all. It takes millions of years for light to travel from the Sun's core to its surface!

130 **Did you know that the name 'Sun' comes from Sun-Sol, the name ancient Romans used for the Sun God?** Thus, the commonly used term, Solar System, means the system of the Sun. Like Ra in ancient Egypt, Sun-Sol occupied a dominant space among the high Gods of Rome.

131 The Sun is a medium-sized star and categorised as a G2 dwarf because of its size, heat and chemical makeup. A G2 star has a complex chemistry which means it includes chemicals which are heavier than helium. It has a temperature which ranges from 5,000-6,000 degree Celsius.

SOLAR SYSTEM

132 Do you know how much we would weigh on the Sun? If a person weighs 150 pounds on Earth, their weight would be 4200 pounds on the Sun. The reason behind this is that the Sun's gravity is 28 times stronger than the Earth's gravity.

133 Have you heard of the solar maximum? It is the period during which there is an increase in solar activities, usually seen every 11 years. During this time, the Sun exchanges its magnetic polarity. This means that the north magnetic pole becomes the south pole and vice versa. The sunspots that are on the Sun explode, hurtling massive clouds of gas known as CMEs through the Solar System.

134 Evidence shows that fluctuation in solar activity can affect the climate on Earth. However, as per most climate scientists and astrophysicists, the Sun is not the cause of the present increase in global temperatures on the Earth. That is a result of human activity.

135 **Did you know that the energy radiated from the Sun changes?** The changes measured are usually very small—scientist have measured that the output changes from one decade to the next by only about one-tenth of one per cent. The changes are not large enough to greatly affect the Earth's weather conditions.

136 **From 1645 to 1715, astronomers observed that sunspots became exceedingly rare.** This came to be known as the Maunder Minimum. This event took place at the same time as the 'Little Ice Age', a 350-year cold spell that had gripped Europe and North America. According to recent calculations, if another Maunder Minimum were to occur, it may result in a decrease of the average temperature on Earth.

137 **Do you know that one day the Sun will be the same size as the Earth?** By the time the Sun has completed its Red Giant phase, it will collapse. It will retain its mass, but become dense, with the same volume as that of the Earth. When this happens, the Sun will become a white dwarf star.

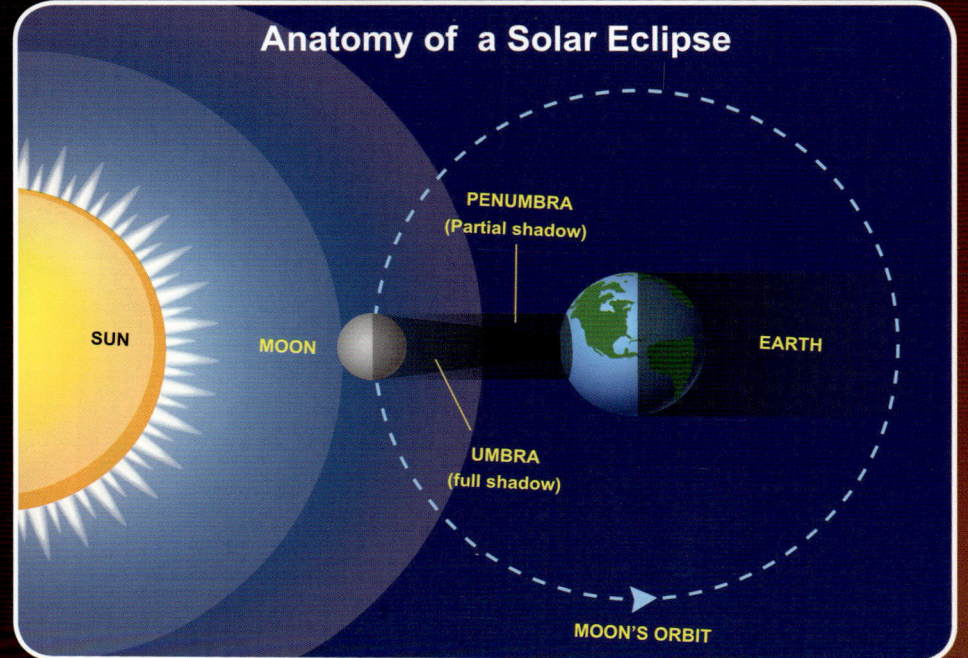

138 **Do you know what is a solar eclipse?** It occurs when the Moon passes in front of the Sun and casts a shadow on the Earth. The Moon is much smaller than the Sun, but because the distance between the Sun and the Earth is about 400 times the distance between the Moon and the Sun, therefore, the Moon appears big enough to block out the Sun. The eclipse is also known as an 'occultation'.

139 **Do you know that the diameter of the Sun is approximately 400 times larger than that of Moon?** However, when seen from the Earth, they seem to be of the same size. This is due to the difference in the distance between the Sun and the Earth and the Moon and the Earth.

140 It is estimated that each year, two to five solar eclipses occur across the world. These can be of three types: partial, annular and total solar eclipse. Do you know that there is another type of solar eclipse? It is known as a hybrid eclipse, and keeps on shifting between a total and annular eclipse depending on where we see it from the Earth. However, such a type of eclipse is very rare.

141 When the Moon does not line up fully with the Sun, it partially blocks the sunlight from reaching the Earth. This causes a partial solar eclipse. Have you heard of the Saros Cycle? It is a period of approximately 18 years, 11 days and 8 hours, when eclipses seem to repeat themselves.

142 Annular solar eclipse occurs when the Moon and the Sun are exactly in line, but either the Moon is far away from the Earth or the Earth is closer to the Sun. When this happens, the size of the Moon appears to be smaller than the Sun. Thus, when it covers the Sun, the edge of the Sun is visible, making it look like a bright ring in the sky.

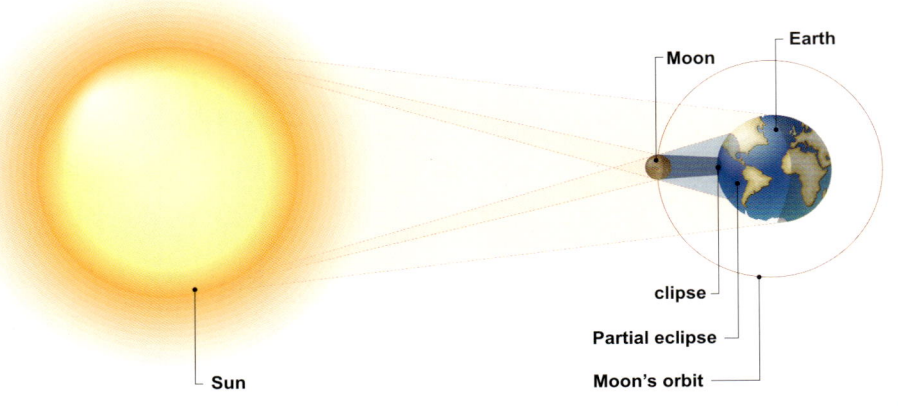

SOLAR ECLIPSE

Moon — Earth — clipse — Partial eclipse — Moon's orbit — Sun

143 **A total solar eclipse occurs when the dark side of the Moon entirely covers the bright light of the Sun.** It can last a maximum of 7 minutes and 30 seconds. During this time, only the faint solar corona can be seen. These solar eclipses are very rare and occur only once every 18 months.

144 **Do you know that the Sun is an average star?** This means that there are many other stars which are cooler or hotter than the Sun. However, it looks bigger and brighter than any other star because it is the closest star to the Earth. The Sun is neither solid nor gaseous. It is in the form of plasma. This means it is gaseous near the surface, but gets denser towards the core.

145 **As you already know, the outer layer of the Sun and other stars is called the corona.** It gets heated up by energies which lead to the corona expanding away from the Sun. This expansion happens in a stream of electrons, protons and atomic particles. This stream can reach a speed of 900 kilometres per second. The solar wind streams, which come from the Sun, can create magnetic disturbances in the Earth's upper atmosphere. This is known as a geomagnetic storm and generates the Southern and Northern Lights (the Aurora).

146 **The corona can get disturbed by the magnetic energy which is produced in the Sun.** This releases tons of solar material and the creates a magnetic field, which are propelled from the Sun into the space at a speed of several million kilometres per hour. These materials expand and widen while moving in space. This is known as a Coronal Mass Ejection (CME) and happens when filaments or prominences become unstable and move away from the Sun.

147 **Have you heard of Solar Energetic Particles (SEPs)?** When a large solar flare or CME takes place, it can produce many atomic particles, electrons, protons and other elements of high energy. These are SEPs. The interesting fact about SEPs is that when they are captured on a camera, they look like a television screen with a lot snow or disturbance!

SOLAR SYSTEM

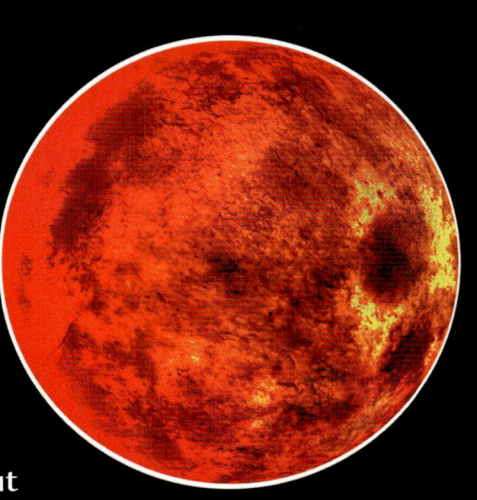

148 **Sunspots are actually the darker but cooler areas on the surface of the Sun.** They occur on the photosphere layer of the Sun and are caused by interactions with the Sun's magnetic field, which have not yet been understood completely. Sunspots are cooler than their surrounding area but appear to be darker.

149 **As a magnetic field has powers of attraction, it holds the plasma from the Sun's chromosphere in the corona.** The filaments from the CMEs are held up in a type of magnetic hammock. The cool filament material becomes dark when seen against the bright solar disk. These filaments can spread across the Sun measuring hundreds of thousands of kilometres. This is equivalent to 10 or more Earths lined together!

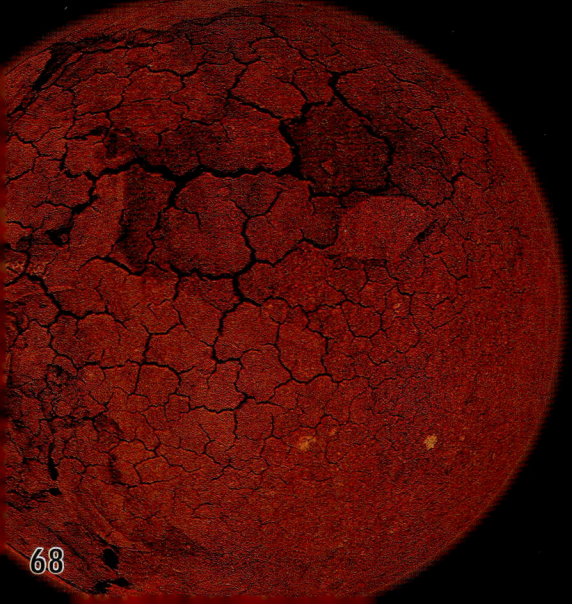

150 **The prominences that flare out from the Sun are bright and gaseous in nature.** These filaments reach out and extend towards outer space. If seen at the side of the Sun's disc, these filaments appear much brighter than the darkness of space. They are anchored in the photosphere and extend out into the corona, often appearing to loop back.

151 **When we observe the Sun under ultraviolet or x-ray light, some dark areas are visible on its surface.** These are called Coronal Holes. These are thought to be the origin points for the high speed solar winds. These holes are mostly found near the Sun's north and south poles, but can occur at other places on the solar disk too. They also have open magnetic fields which helps the coronal material escape.

152 **The Solar Dynamics Observatory (SDO) was the first mission launched by NASA as part of their Living With a Star (LWS) program.** This program was designed to understand what causes solar differences and also study the solar atmosphere. Another objective was to learn how a magnetic field is generated on the Sun and how the stored magnetic energy converts into the heliosphere.

Mercury

153 Mercury is the closest planet to the Sun and is the smallest planet in the Solar System, with a diameter of only 4,879 kilometres. It has no moon or rings. An interesting mystery related to the planet is that till today, nobody knows who first discovered Mercury. One year on Mercury takes place in just 88 Earth days. This is because being closer to the Sun, its orbit is smaller.

154 Mercury has very long days, as it spins very slowly on its axis, as compared to Earth. One day on Mercury takes about 58 days and 15 hours! Due to its proximity to Earth, it is visible to the naked eye. It can be seen generally during twilight. The total mass of the planet is 3.30×10^{23} kilogram which is approximately 5.5 per cent the size of the Earth. The surface temperature of Mercury is -173 degree to 427 degree Celsius.

155 When Mercury passes directly between the Sun and a bigger planet, it is visible against the solar disk. This is called the transit of Mercury. This phenomenon takes place every eight years on an average. From the Earth, scientists and astronomers have observed this phenomenon as many as 13-14 times in a century.

156 One of the most interesting facts about Mercury is that it has the thinnest atmosphere amongst all the known planets. As there is less air or almost no air, sound cannot travel through it, which makes it a very silent planet. Its gravitational force is only 38 per cent of Earth's gravity, which is not enough to hold on to the atmosphere. Thus, the atmosphere can get easily blown away by solar winds.

MERCURY

157 Do you know that it is very difficult to visit Mercury because of its proximity to the Sun? Up till now only two space crafts have gone to Mercury. The first was Mariner 10, which flew by the planet three times in 1974–75, mapping about half the planet's surface. The second was the Messenger probe, which orbited the planet from 2011–13, and mapped the planet completely.

158 Mercury has the most number of craters among all the planets in the Solar System! The surface of this planet is covered by thousands of craters because of collisions with several asteroids and comets. Most of the other planets have a self-healing tendency, which occurs due to natural geological processes. However, Mercury lacks this process. The craters are of different sizes and shapes. A crater larger than 250 kilometres is known as a basin.

159 The largest crater on the surface of Mercury is called the Caloris Basin. Its diameter measures around 1,550 kilometres. This crater was discovered by the Mariner 10 probe in 1974. Did you know, most craters on Mercury are named after well-known writers and artists?

SOLAR SYSTEM

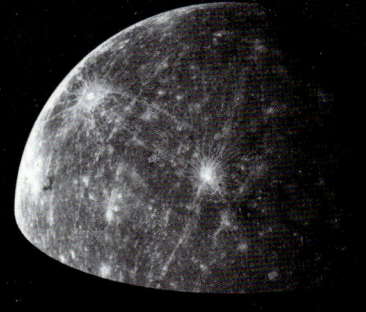

MERCURY CORE

CORE 1800 km
MANTLE 1800 km
CRUST 100-200 km

160 Do you know what Mercury is made up of? Earlier, scientists from NASA used to believe that Mercury consists of a solid iron core, but recent research shows that it most likely has a molten core. This molten core consists of lighter elements like sulphur, which has lowered the melting point of the core. Mercury's core makes up 42 per cent of its volume, in contrast to Earth's 17 per cent.

161 Mercury has wrinkles on its surface, like human beings have on their faces. The iron core of the planet is constantly cooling down and contracting. This is the reason why the surface of the planet becomes wrinkled. The scientists have named these wrinkles 'Lobate Scarps'. These scarps can be as long as a mile high and hundreds of miles long.

MERCURY

DISTANCE FROM THE SUN: 57 910 000 km
RADIUS: 2 440 km
SURFACE AREA: 74 800 000 km2
DAY LENGTH: 58d 15h 30 min
ORBITAL PERIOD: 88 days
SURFACE TEMPERATURE: 180 to 430⁰C
MOONS: 0

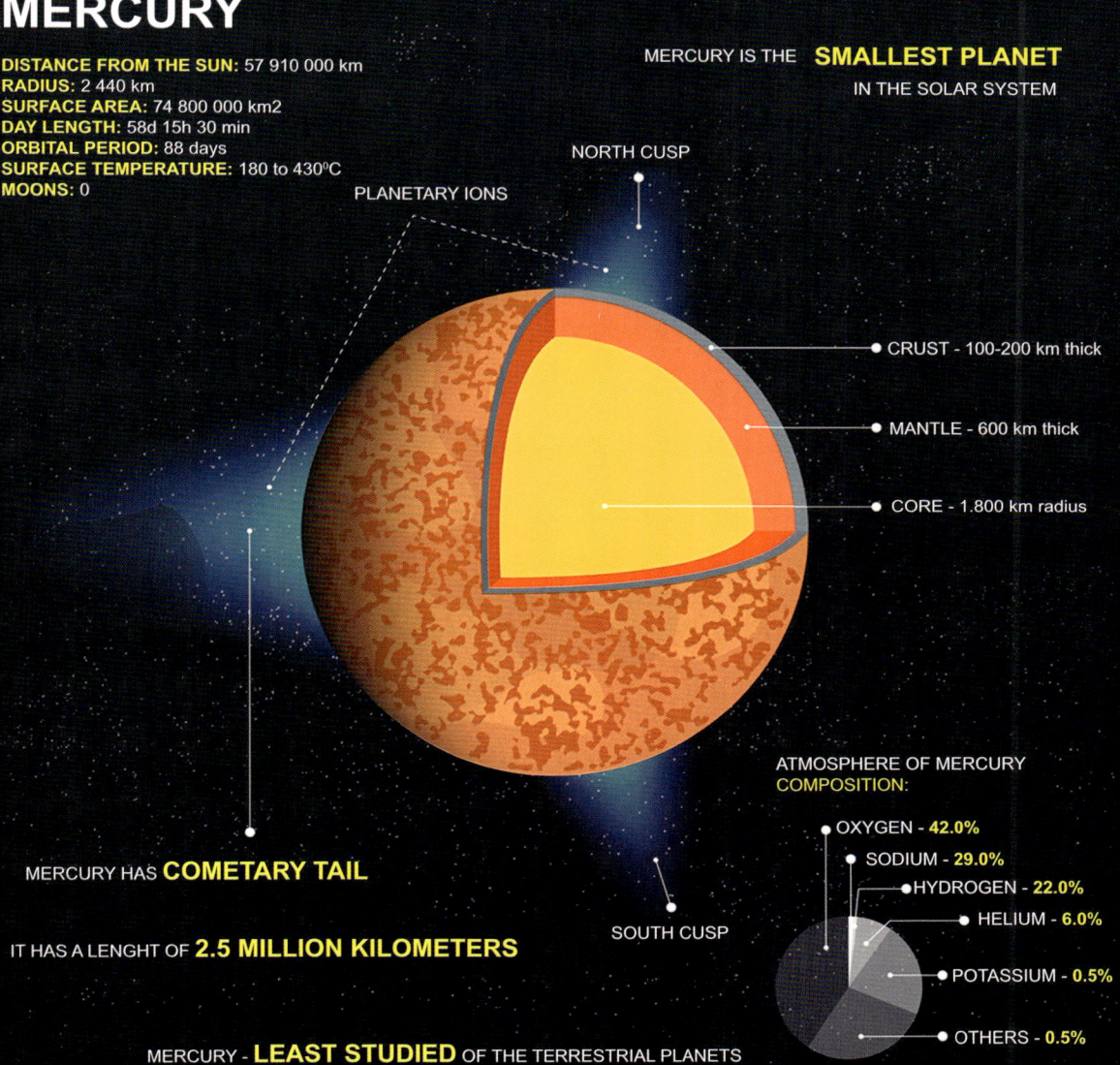

MERCURY IS THE **SMALLEST PLANET** IN THE SOLAR SYSTEM

NORTH CUSP
PLANETARY IONS
CRUST - 100-200 km thick
MANTLE - 600 km thick
CORE - 1.800 km radius

ATMOSPHERE OF MERCURY COMPOSITION:
OXYGEN - **42.0%**
SODIUM - **29.0%**
HYDROGEN - **22.0%**
HELIUM - **6.0%**
POTASSIUM - **0.5%**
OTHERS - **0.5%**

SOUTH CUSP

MERCURY HAS **COMETARY TAIL**
IT HAS A LENGTH OF **2.5 MILLION KILOMETERS**

MERCURY - **LEAST STUDIED** OF THE TERRESTRIAL PLANETS

162

Mercury is very dense despite the small size of the planet. Each cubic centimetre of the planet contains a density of 5.4 grams. Mercury is the second densest planet in the Solar System after the Earth. The reason behind its density is that it is mainly composed of heavy metals and rocks. The surprising thing is that our weight on Mercury would be just 38 per cent of the weight we exhibit on the Earth.

SOLAR SYSTEM

163 **Among all the planets, Mercury has the highest orbital eccentricity.** Orbital eccentricity means the amount an astronomical object deviates from a perfect circle. Mercury's distance from the Sun can thus range from anywhere from 46 to 70 million kilometres. It takes around 87.96 Earth days for it complete an orbit of the Sun.

164 **We still know very little about how Mercury was formed.** The spacecraft, Mariner 10, gave us a lot of information about its surface. However, a lot needs to be explored about this unique planet, which is considered to hold many answers about the origin of all our planets.

Venus

165 **Venus is the second planet from the Sun.** It has a mass of 4.87 x 10^24 kg, which is around 81.5 per cent the size of the Earth. Do you know that Venus is named after the Roman goddess of love and beauty? After the Sun and Moon, Venus is the second brightest object in the sky and can be seen easily by the naked eye.

166 **An interesting fact about Venus is that it is the second largest terrestrial planet and is often known as Earth's sister planet because of their similar size and mass.** The surface of Venus consists of layers of clouds containing sulphuric acid. Mainly, it is made up of an iron core, rocky mantle and silicate crust. It has a surface temperature of 462 degree Celsius.

167 **Venus does not have any moons or any rings.** Do you know that one day on Venus is longer than a year? A solar day on its surface takes 117 Earth days. Its orbit around the Sun is equivalent to 225 Earth days. It is as big as Earth, with a diameter of 12,104 kilometres.

SOLAR SYSTEM

168 **You would be surprised to know that Venus rotates in a direction opposite to most other planets.** While most planets rotate on their axes in the anti-clockwise direction, Venus rotates clockwise in retrograde rotation, once every 243 Earth days. The reason behind such alteration in its path could be a collision with an asteroid or some other object in the past.

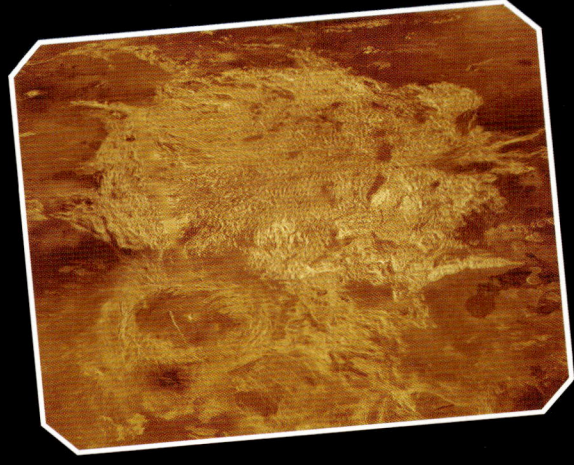

169 **Do you know that atmospheric pressure on Venus is 92 times higher than on Earth?** This is despite their size, mass and density being identical. Unlike Mercury, Venus has no craters on its surface. The pressure it exercises is the same as experienced under the sea on Earth.

VENUS

DISTANCE FROM THE SUB: 108 200 000 km
RADIUS: 6 052 km
SURFACE AREA: 460 200 000 km2
DAY LENGTH: 116d 18h 0 min
ORBITAL PERIOD: 224,7 days
SURFACE TEMPERATURE: 460°C
MOONS: 0

SUN ON VENUS
RISES IN **THE WEST** AND SETS IN **THE EAST**

- CRUST - 50 km thick
- MANTLE - 3000 km thick
- CORE

ATMOSPHERE OF VENUS
COMPOSITION:
- CARBON DIOXIDE - **96.5%**
- NITROGEN - **3.5%**

NEAR THE SURFACE OF THE PLANET WAS
6 AMERICAN SPACECRAFT AND **18 SOVIET**

ON VENUS, IT RAINS **SULPHURIC ACID**

170 The surface of Venus experiences no temperature variation because of which Venus doesn't have seasons. Everywhere on Venus the temperature remains the same, averaging 460 degree Celsius. This is because unlike Earth, Venus is not tilted or inclined on its axis. The other reason is because the thick atmosphere, which contains carbon dioxide, traps the heat and distributes it across the planet uniformly.

SOLAR SYSTEM

171 Over the years, Venus has been known by other names as well. Two of these are 'Morning Star' and 'Evening Star'. Earlier, people used to believe that Venus was actually two different celestial bodies. These two bodies were named Phosphorus and Hesperus by the Greeks and Lucifer and Vesper by the Romans.

172 An elaborate research on Venus was carried out by the Mayan astronomers in early 650 CE. Do you know that there are more than 1,000 volcanic points on Venus? Each volcanic point can be as large as 20 kilometres. To know more about the planet, the European Space Agency (ESA) sent the Venus Express Space Shuttle to orbit around the planet and collect information about it, from 2005–14.

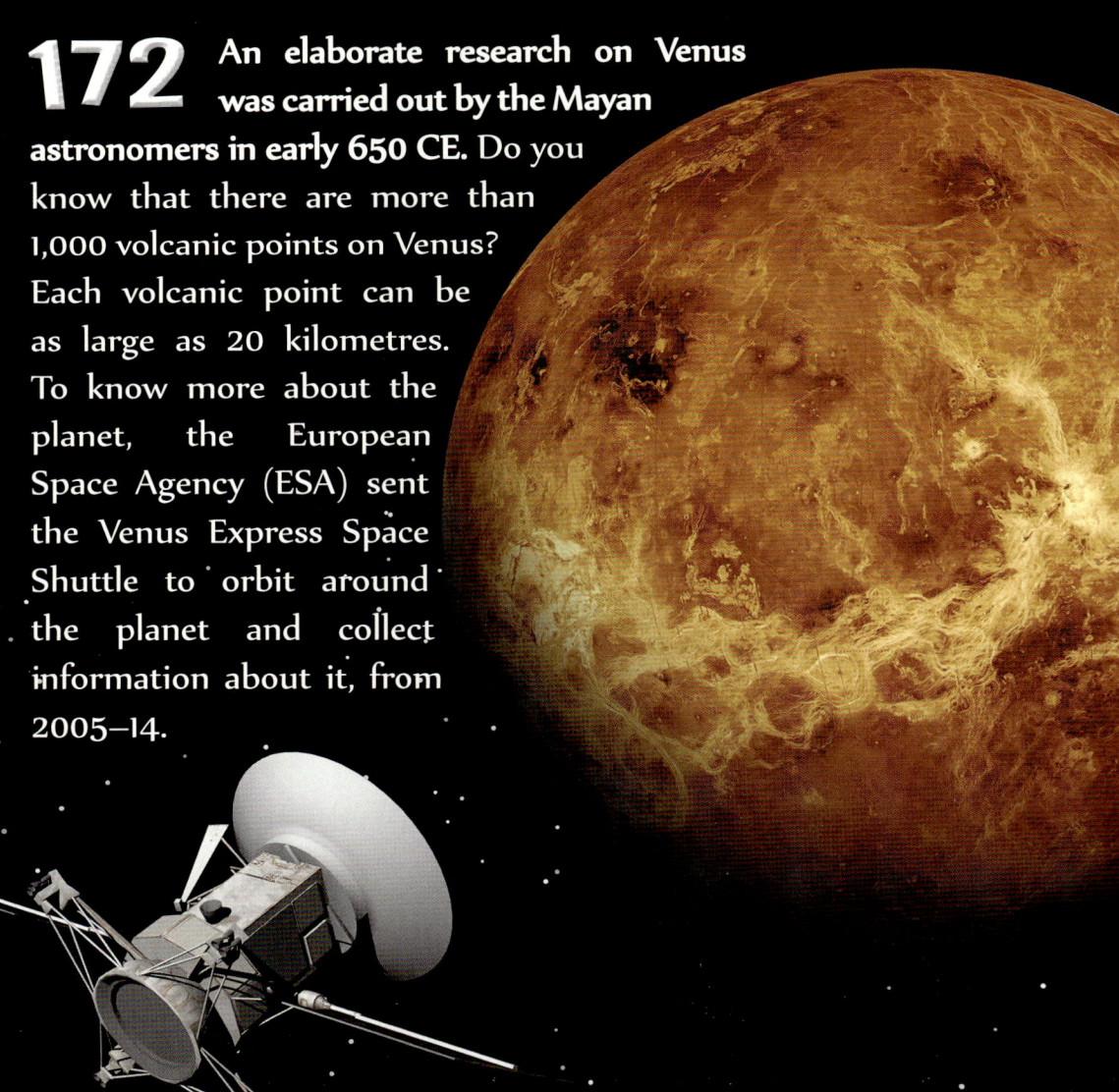

VENUS

173 Can you imagine Venus having oceans? It is believed that there was a time when Venus had oceans. However, with increasing temperature, the oceans disappeared. Around the 1960s, through radio mapping, scientists could determine the temperature and environmental conditions of the planet. They found that the view of Venus's surface is not very clear due to clouds of sulphuric acid that are present in its atmosphere.

174 No one can ever think about visiting Venus because of its harsh atmospheric conditions. It consists of a thick yellow-white cloud of sulphuric acid gas which is very harmful. Moreover, the surface temperature is 100 times higher than that of the Earth. This intense heat would not allow anyone to survive there for even a second.

175 **Till now, 38 spacecrafts have been sent to Venus.** The first mission was sent by the Russians in 1961. The Russian Venera 1 space probe was followed by the US probe, Mariner 1. However, both these attempts were not successful. However, in 1962, Mariner 2 was more successful in bringing back the planet's measurements.

176 **'Venera' is the Russian name for Venus.** Between 1961 and 1984, the Soviet Union sent a series of Venera space probes to gather data from Venus. Most of these revealed that the surface of Venus is a hot desert with many small lowlands and highlands. When Venus moves across the face of the Sun, it is known as a Venus transit. It has been predicted that the next Venus transit will occur on December 10 and 11, 2117. The last one was recorded on June 5 and 6, 2012.

Earth

177 The Earth, our home, is the third planet from the Sun. Of the four terrestrial planets—Mercury, Venus, Earth and Mars—Earth is the largest one. A terrestrial planet is one which is mainly made up of rocks and metals. Earth is also the only one that has the necessary conditions, like oxygen, oceans and seas, which support life.

178 The Earth was formed around 4.54 billion years ago. This planet has unique features which are not found on any other planet in our Solar System. It is also the only planet in our Solar System which is not named after any Greek or Roman deity.

SOLAR SYSTEM

179 The presence of water and other conditions which support life have transformed Earth from a molten planet to its present form. The evolution of life forms has helped to produce the present atmosphere. The Earth's atmosphere consists largely of nitrogen and oxygen, which in turn provide suitable conditions to sustain life.

180 Do you know that Earth is not a perfect sphere? While the poles are flattened, the equator bulges out. In the case of the Earth, the reason behind this bulge is due to its rotation. As the Earth keeps moving, gravity is concentrated towards the centre and in return a force pushes outward.

181 How and when was the Earth formed? Earth is relatively young and was formed along with other planets about 4,600 million years ago. In the beginning, Earth was very cold and covered with ice. However, radioactivity heated it up until the ice melted. The iron rocks which were heavy sank to the centre and the lighter rocks floated to the top. At present, the Earth's molten core is surrounded by a fluid mantle of rock.

EARTH

182 **Earth reflects about one-third of the sunlight which falls on it.** The light scatters and makes our plant appear largely blue-coloured from space. The surface crust on which we live is only a few miles thick. Around 2/3rd of the Earth's area is covered with water, of which the Pacific Ocean covers almost half the globe.

183 Did you know the Earth is made up of more than one layer? There are three main layers—the crust, the mantle and the core. The most interesting part about its layers is the inner most layer (the core), which is extremely hot. In fact, the outer core is liquid in state!

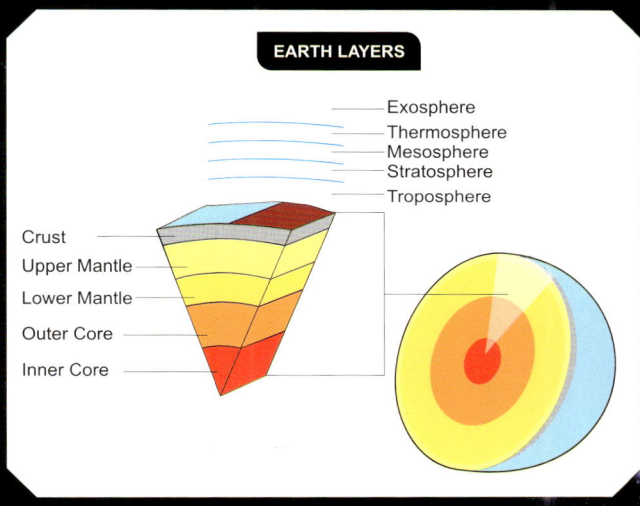

184 **Earth is the only planet with tectonic plates.** This means that its surface doesn't stay stable. But what is tectonic plate? The Earth's crust is broken up into regions which are known as tectonic plates. These plates float on top of the magma at the core of the Earth. When two plates collide, it results in the formation of a fresh crust. These geological activities cause earthquakes.

185 Do you know that the Earth recycles itself? Earth's rock cycle is such that it transforms the igneous rocks to sedimentary rocks to metamorphic rocks and back again. The leftover rocks, rich in carbons, are carried to the interior of the Earth and recycled. This recycling of carbon would not be possible without the action of tectonic plates. Without them Earth would overheat and burn.

186 Do you know the hottest spot on Earth? It is El Azizia in Libya. Temperature there can go as high as 57.8 degree Celsius. This high temperature was recorded on 14 September 1922 by NASA's Earth Observatory. The data was collected by the Moderate Resolution Imaging Spectroradiometer (MODIS). However, there could be other regions which are hotter than this, but lie beyond the network of the weather stations.

187 As you already know, 70 per cent of the Earth's surface is covered by water. When astronauts first went to space, they saw that the Earth appeared blue. From this, Earth got its nickname, the Blue Planet. The remaining 30 per cent of Earth is the solid, rocky crust, which is situated above sea level and therefore called the Continental Crust.

EARTH

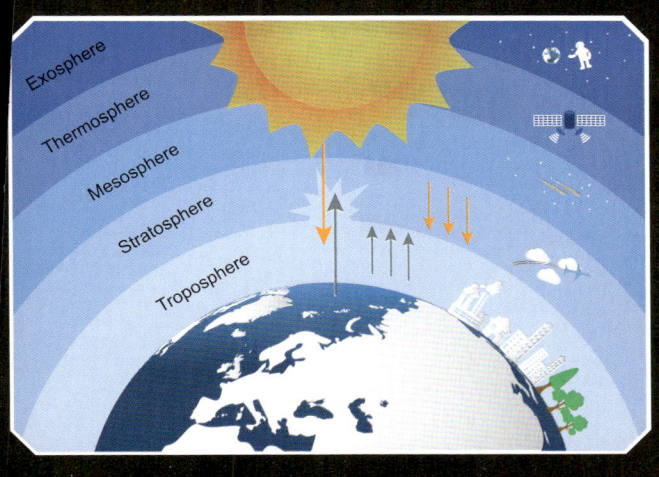

188

The Earth's atmosphere covers 10,000 kilometres, outwards towards space. The atmosphere is thickest within the first 50 km from the surface, before finally reaching out into space. It is made up of five layers: Troposphere, Stratosphere, Mesosphere, Thermosphere and Exosphere. Air pressure and density decreases the higher one goes into the atmosphere and the farther one is from the surface.

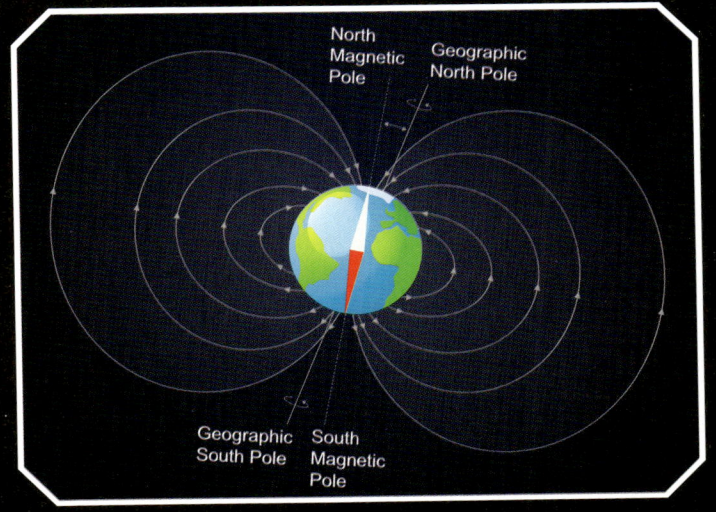

189

Did you know that the Earth's molten iron core creates a magnetic field? How does it do that? The Earth is like a big magnet, with its two poles located in the north and south. The magnetic field thus created by Earth spreads over thousands of kilometres from its surface and forms a region called the 'magnetosphere'. Particles from the Sun's solar winds do not directly hit the Earth because of this magnetosphere.

SOLAR SYSTEM

190 The Earth has one natural satellite, the Moon. The Moon is the fifth largest natural satellite in our Solar System. 3753 Cruithne and 2002 AA29 are two asteroids in its co-orbital orbit which are a part of a larger population of asteroids known as Near-Earth Objects (NEOs). Objects that have a co-orbital orbit basically follow the same orbit around the Sun and are thus closely related to the planet.

191 Earth has a total mass of 5.97×10^{24} kilograms. It has a polar diameter of 12,714 kilometres and an equatorial diameter of 12,756 kilometres. Earth is the densest planet of all the planets in the Solar System. The average density of the Earth is around 5.52 grams per cubic centimetre. However, density can vary according to the composition of that particular region of the planet. For example, the metallic core is denser than the crust.

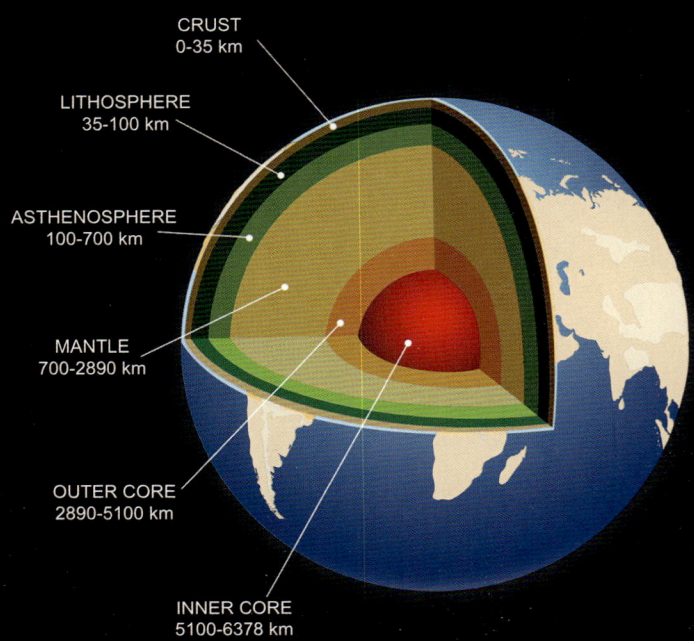

EARTH STRUCTURE

CRUST
0-35 km

LITHOSPHERE
35-100 km

ASTHENOSPHERE
100-700 km

MANTLE
700-2890 km

OUTER CORE
2890-5100 km

INNER CORE
5100-6378 km

192 **Do you know that the Earth's rotation is gradually slowing down?** It has been calculated that the rotational speed is decreasing by 17 milliseconds every one hundred years. However, the rate of decrease is not uniform. Its impact can be seen by the lengthening of the days. However, it is happening very slowly and scientists estimate that it would be as much as 140 million years before the length of a day will increase to 25 hours.

193 **Did you know that the coldest spot on Earth can be found in Antarctica?** In winters, temperature can go down to -73.3 degree Celsius. According to the records of the United States Geological Survey (USGS), on July 21, 1983, Russia's Vostok Station reached a temperature of -89 degree Celsius, the lowest ever recorded temperature.

194 **Do you know that at one time, Earth was believed to be the centre of the Universe?** Ancient astronomers believed that the Earth was fixed and the other celestial bodies revolved around it in circular orbits. They thought so because of what they perceived to be the movement of the Sun and other planets. In 1543, Copernicus proved that actually the Sun was at the centre and Earth along with the other celestial bodies moved around it.

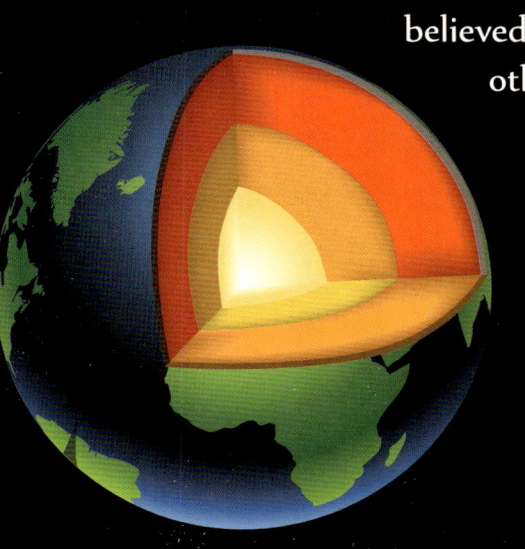

195 It is believed that Earth was not alone in its orbit around the Sun. According to research by scientists, at one point, Earth had a twin planet called Theia. Theia would have been the size of Mars and was 60 degrees either in front or behind Earth. Theia is believed to have crashed into the Earth and most of it absorbed into Earth. However, it left some chunks behind, which combined with other materials from our planet formed the Moon.

196 The earliest life form developed in the oceans by a process called abiogenesis or biopoiesis. This is a natural process in which life grows from non-living matter like simple organic compounds, such as bacteria or fungi.

197 Earth is covered by an ozone layer which helps in protecting it from harmful solar radiation. It acts like a protective shell surrounding the Earth. The shell is made of a special type of oxygen which absorbs most of the Sun's powerful ultra-violet rays. These rays can be very harmful for our skin and eyes.

EARTH

198 There are a few visible craters found on the surface of the Earth. The craters are fewer in number as compared with the other bodies in our Solar System. The reason behind this is that Earth is geologically active, and processes like movement of its tectonic plates and erosion constantly reshape its surface.

199 At a height of 8, 848 metres, Mount Everest is the highest point on Earth. It is over 60 million years old. Everest was formed by the movement of the Indian tectonic plate pushing up and against the Asian plate. The lowest point on the Earth is known as Challenger Deep, which is 10.9 meters below sea level. It is part of the Mariana Trench in the Pacific Ocean.

200 Do you know that the Earth has one of the most circular orbits? Further, its axis of rotation is tilted 23.4 degree away from the right angle of its orbital plane and this produces the seasons we experience.

SOLAR SYSTEM

201 Do you know which is the softest known mineral found on Earth? It is called 'talc'. It is used in a variety of ways, like such as glaze in ceramics and as a filler in paper. Even the talcum powder we use is made from it. This mineral is composed of hydrated magnesium silicate.

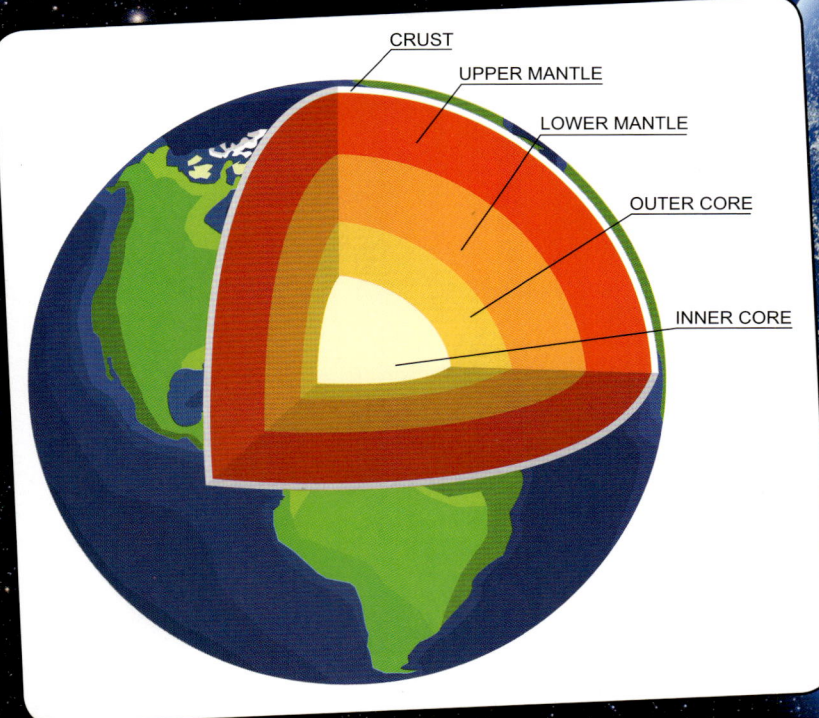

202 The centre of the Earth, also known as the core, mainly contains iron and nickel. The inner core is solid and measures 1,220 kilometres in diameter. The outer core is molten, liquid metal. Together, the inner core and outer core are about as big as Mars. The diameter of the outer core is 2266 kilometres.

EARTH

203 **The Earth's crust is made of granite and other solid rock material.** Sand, soil and crushed rock have settled on top of the crust. The crust's width ranges from five to 64 kilometres. While the mantle of the Earth is solid rock, it is not entirely hard. It runs approximately 2900 kilometres deep.

204 **Do you know about Moving Rocks?** Since the early 1900s, Death Valley in California has experienced a natural phenomenon in which rocks and even huge boulders move along with the dry lake bed. The movement may be tiny, just a few inches, or could be more than 3,000 feet. Though no one has seen these rocks move, one can observe the pattern of movements left behind, which are evidence of this movement.

205 **The Earth's surface is never constant. It varies from time to time and place to place.** This is because soil is eroded and shifted by wind, water and rain. It takes almost 500 to 1,000 years to replenish one inch of topsoil after it has been eroded. The soil holds nearly .01 per cent of the Earth's water, which it has absorbed.

SOLAR SYSTEM

206 As per research, the oldest known rocks on Earth are the Nuvvuagittuq Greenstone Belt on the coast of Hudson Bay in Northern Quebec. These rocks are 4.28 billion years old. Geologists took samples to estimate the age of the rocks. These rocks were isolated from mineral grains called zircons, which are very resistant to weathering and geologic processes.

207 Do you know about the deepest man-made hole? It can be found in the Kola peninsula of Russia. Known as the Kola Superdeep Borehole, it is the result of a scientific drilling project. The attempt was to drill as deep as possible into the Earth's crust. It is as deep as 12,226 metres. However, this distinction now belongs to an oil well in Qatar, which is 12,289 metres deep. While digging into the Earth, scientists have realised just how thick each layer of the Earth is.

208 The crust and the mantle are divided by a boundary known as the Mohorovicic discontinuity (Moho). This boundary got its name from Andrija Mohorovicic, who discovered it in 1910. Another discovery made by him was that the earthquake waves changed when they passed through the two layers.

EARTH

209 Due to the intense heat from the crust, the mantle is mouldable, just like dough. As a result, the mantle also moves. This movement causes earthquakes and volcanic eruptions. The temperature at the core is hotter than the Sun's surface. The movement of material deep inside the Earth also generates the Earth's magnetic field, which is known as the magnetosphere.

210 What is Global Warming? It refers to an increase in Earth's average surface temperature because of the greenhouse gas effect. Gases such as carbon dioxide and methane are increasing in the Earth's atmosphere. They absorb and retain heat which would have otherwise escaped from the Earth. It has created one of the biggest environmental issues in the past few decades. According to the inter-governmental Panel on Climate Change (IPCC) report in 2007, the sea levels will rise seven to 23 inches by the end of the century due to global warming.

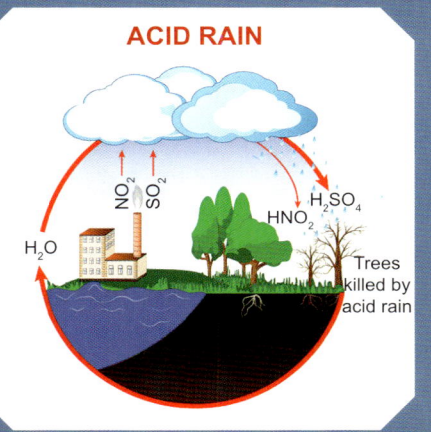

ACID RAIN

211 Another environmental hazard Earth is experiencing is acid rain. This term is used for different types of acidic air pollution. These air pollutants fall back to the Earth in the form of rain, snow, sleet, hail, mist or fog. Therefore, it is known as acid rain. This contains chemicals such as sulphur dioxide and nitrogen oxides. Sometimes, chemicals fall directly on the ground. This is called dry deposition.

212 As you know, the Earth's atmosphere has different layers. The lowest region, the troposphere, extends from its surface up to about 10 to 12 kilometres. The stratosphere goes from 2 kilometres to about 50 kilometres. Most of the atmospheric ozone is situated in this layer. Above it lies the mesosphere. It extends upward to a height of about 80 kilometres above our planet. The layer of very rare, thin air above the mesosphere is called the thermosphere.

213 What is ozone? It is an inorganic molecule which contains three atoms of oxygen. It is blue in colour and has a strong odour. Ozone is different from the normal oxygen we breathe. Out of every 10 million air molecules, around two million are normal oxygen and only three are ozone.

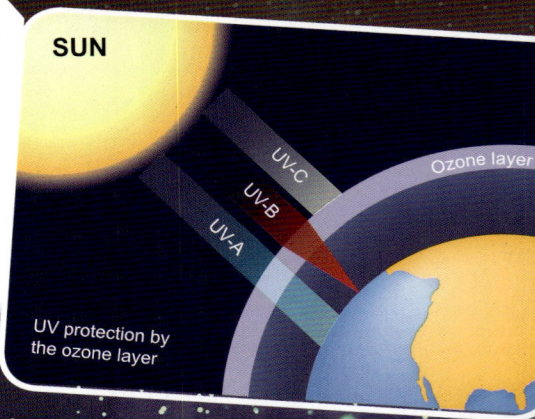

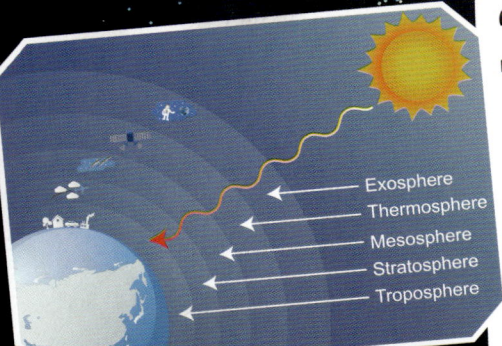

214 Is ozone important in the atmosphere? Yes, it is. Even a small amount of ozone plays a very important role in our atmosphere. The ozone layer absorbs a part of the radiation from the Sun and prevents it from reaching Earth. The most useful thing which it absorbs is ultraviolet light called UVB, which can be harmful for us.

215 The ultraviolet rays which enter the Earth's surface are very harmful. They can cause various types of skin cancer, cataract problems and even damage crops and marine life. They are also capable of damaging and destroying the various layers of the Earth's atmosphere.

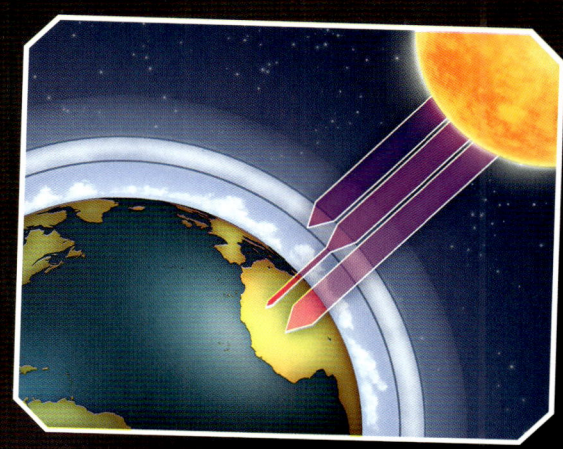

216 How is ozone depleted? It is caused by the release of chlorofluorocarbons (CFCs) and other ozone-depleting substances (ODS). They are stable, non-flammable, low in toxicity and inexpensive to produce. These CFCs are used as refrigerants, solvents, foam blowing agents and other smaller applications. They release chlorine or bromine when they break down, which can damage the protective ozone layer. CFCs are stable and do not dissolve in rain, making them even more dangerous.

217 Have you ever wondered if natural sources are also responsible for the depletion of the ozone layer? Though volcanoes and oceans release large amounts of chlorine, which reduces ozone, these can easily dissolve in water and wash out of the atmosphere in the form of rain. It is the man-made CFCs which do not dissolve in water.

SOLAR SYSTEM

218 **It is important to have the correct amount of ozone in the atmosphere.** We cannot make enough ozone to replace what has already been destroyed, but we can stop producing ozone depleting substances. By 2050, natural ozone production reactions must be brought back, to bring the ozone layer to its normal level.

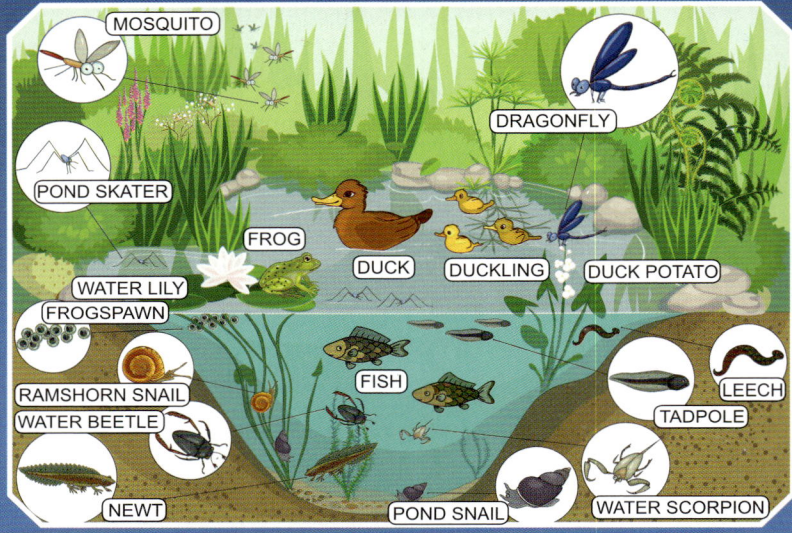

219 **The part of the Earth where life exists is known as the biosphere.** Within the biosphere, there are many smaller ecosystems. Ecosystems can be as small as raindrops or as big as oceans. An ecosystem contains group of living beings surviving together.

220 **Cyanobacteria are the oldest fossils present on Earth.** They are unicellular and lack a nucleus. Being the largest group of bacteria, they are found on land and in brackish or marine water. They use sunlight to produce their own food.

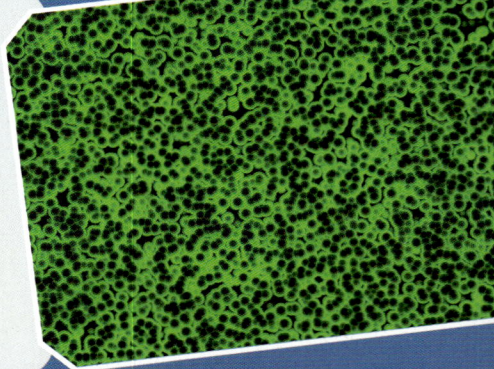

EARTH

221 The length of a year is fixed according to the Earth's average orbital distance of 1.50 x 108 km. With an orbital eccentricity of .0167, the Earth's orbit is one of the most circular in all the Solar System. The reason behind this is very small difference between the Earth's perihelion and aphelion, that is, the nearest and the farthest points of a body's direct orbit around the Sun.

222 Because of the small difference between the perihelion and aphelion of the Earth's orbit, we receive different amounts of sunlight at different times of the year. Therefore, Earth's position in its orbit is responsible for the variation in the seasons we experience. The Earth's axial tilt is approximately 23.45 degree. The effect of this tilt is that the amount of sunlight the northern hemisphere receives is greater than what the southern hemisphere receives during one half of the year, and vice versa during the second half of the year.

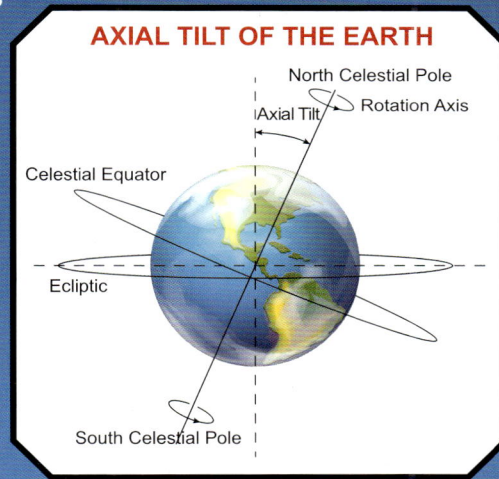

AXIAL TILT OF THE EARTH

223 Do you know the reason for the existence of the oceans? One main reason is that the Earth itself had large amounts of water vapour trapped under its surface during its formation. Geological movements like volcanic activity released this water vapour into the atmosphere where this vapour condensed, falling back to the Earth's surface as liquid water.

224 Earth is the only planet in the Solar System where water is present in all three states: solid, liquid and vapour. Another reason for the existence of oceans on Earth is supposed to be the ancient comets that struck the Earth. It is believed that they deposited some amounts of water in the form of ice on the planet.

225 You already know how the Earth's position determines the climate of an area. The other factors which determine climate and the seasons are distance from the equator, oceanic currents and distance from the sea. Some areas which are small have their own climatic conditions known as a microclimate.

226 Around six per cent of the Earth's surface is occupied by wetlands. They are the largest producer of plant material on Earth. They even provide refuge to birds, who feel safe there because there are fewer predatory animals. Wetlands consist wet grasslands called marshes; wet peat lands called bogs; and waterlogged forests called swamps.

Moon

227 **The Moon is a spherical body made up of hard rocks and is covered with dust.** It is the only natural satellite of Earth. Its surface is full of craters. It was formed some 30–50 million years after the formation of our Solar System. The size of the Moon is one-quarter the size of the Earth.

228 **The Moon moves in synchronous rotation with the Earth, which means that the Earth only ever gets to see one side of the Moon.** The total mass of the Moon is 7.35×10^{22} kilogram. It has a surface temperature of 233 degree to 123 degree Celsius and has a diameter of 3,475 kilometres. The Moon revolves around the Earth.

229 **The rise and the fall of tides on Earth is caused by the Moon.** It is interesting to note that every year the Moon is actually moving approximately 3.8 centimetres away from the Earth. It is predicted that this movement will continue for at least 50 billion years more. If this happens, the Moon will take around 47 days to move around the Earth instead of the current 27.3 days.

230 **There is a myth that the side of the Moon we cannot see is dark.** The truth is that both sides of the Moon receive the same amount of sunlight. However, since only one side of the Moon is visible from the Earth, we think the other side lies in darkness. The reason behind this is that the Moon rotates on its own axis in the same time it takes to orbit the Earth. The side which is not visible from Earth can thus only be seen from a spacecraft.

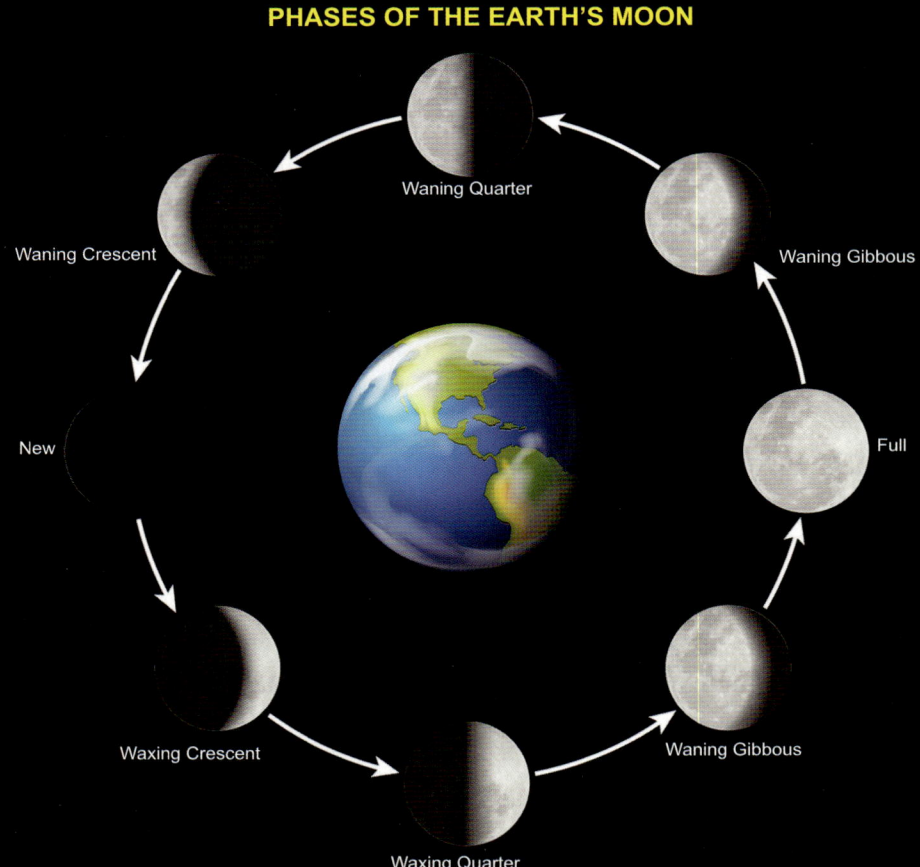

PHASES OF THE EARTH'S MOON

231 **The Latin term 'Luna' is associated with the Moon.** It was used for the Roman Goddess of the Moon. Today, the term has led to derivatives like 'lunar', when we talk about the Moon, for instance, lunar calendar, lunar eclipse, and so on.

232 How much do you think a person weighs on the Moon? As the Moon has weaker gravity as compared with Earth due to its smaller mass, a person will weigh less on the Moon. The weight will be about one sixth (16.5 per cent) of the person's weight on the Earth. This is the reason why astronauts who have gone to the Moon could leap and bound high in the air while walking on the Moon.

233

According to astronauts who have visited the Moon, it also experiences quakes. This is because it has a molten core under its surface, just like the Earth. Astronauts used seismographs while visiting the Moon and measured these small moonquakes. These quakes may also be caused due to the gravitational pull of the Earth. The ruptures and cracks on the surface of Moon are a result of these quakes.

234 **The Moon has a very thin and weak atmosphere and is therefore vulnerable to cosmic rays, meteorites and solar winds.** This also accounts for the huge temperature variations that it experiences. This almost complete lack of atmosphere also gives Moon another unique characteristic. No sound can be heard on the Moon because there is not enough air to carry the sound waves. The sky above the Moon also always appears black as the atmosphere is not dense enough to refract light like on Earth.

SOLAR SYSTEM

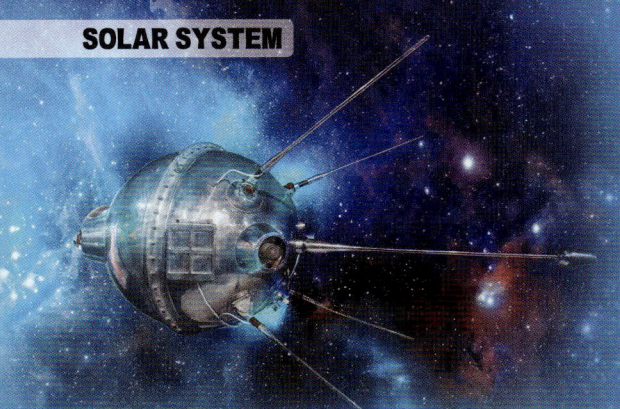

235 The first spacecraft to Moon was Luna 1 in 1959. It was the first unmanned mission to the Moon launched by the USSR. This spacecraft passed within 599 kilometres of the surface of the Moon before going into orbit around the Sun. The first manned shuttle was NASA's Apollo 11, which landed on the Moon in 1969.

236 Earth's Moon is much smaller than the moons of Jupiter and Saturn. Even so, it is the fifth largest satellite. According to scientists, the Moon may have once been a part of the Earth itself, which broke away, or it might have been part of Theia, which could have collided with the Earth years ago.

237 NASA plans to send another expedition to the Moon. This will give astronauts the opportunity to once again walk the Moon's surface in the year 2019. In the process, they would collect samples and study the Moon further.

238 During the 1950s USA had contemplated detonating a nuclear bomb on the Moon! This project was planned during the Cold War era and was called 'A Study of Lunar Research Flights' or 'Project A119'. The project was top-secret and was meant to symbolise the country's strength because they felt that USSR was overtaking them in the space race.

MOON

239 All planets in the Solar System have moons, except Mercury and Venus. Some, like Jupiter and Saturn, have many moons. In fact, there are about 176 known natural satellites, or moons, in the Solar System.

240 The Moon does not have its own light, but it seems like a very bright object to us because it reflects sunlight. You must have noticed that the Moon doesn't always have the same shape or size when we see it in the sky. This is because it goes through different phrases. These are: new moon, waxing crescent, first quarter, waxing gibbous, full moon, waning gibbous, third quarter, and waning crescent.

241 Do you know how wide the Moon is? The Moon has a diameter of 3,474 kilometres. Its surface area is equivalent to the surface area of Africa! Like the Earth, its surface is covered with craters, lava plains, mountains and valleys.

SOLAR SYSTEM

242 A Blue Moon is a phenomenon that happens when two full moons occur within one calendar month. On an average, such a situation occurs once every three years. The last Blue Moon occurred on July 31, 2015. Before that, Blue Moons were seen on December 31, 2009 and August 31, 2012. The phrase 'once in a blue moon' is thus used to describe a very rare situation.

243

There are several mountains on Moon. The tallest mountain on the Moon is Mons Huygens with a height of 5,500 metres. Several samples of Moon rocks were brought back to Earth. After studying these rocks, scientists have learnt a lot about the composition of the Moon.

244 Sometimes when viewed from the Earth, the Moon appears to be surrounded by a ring of light. This is called the Lunar Halo. It is formed when light is refracted through ice crystals in cirrus clouds. These ice crystals have six sides which refract the light at a 22 degree angle.

245 Do you know how many people have walked on the Moon? So far 12 people—men, all from the United States—have walked across the face of the Moon. The first man who touched the Moon's surface was Neil Armstrong in 1969. The last man was Gene Cernan in 1972 on the Apollo 17 Mission. Since then, the Moon has been visited only by unmanned vehicles.

246 A lunar month is the amount of time the Moon takes to pass through a complete cycle of all its phases. The lunar month is calculated by measuring the size of the Moon, beginning from one New Moon to the next New Moon. A lunar month has around 29.5 days, which means it is longer than the number of days it takes the Moon to complete an orbit around the Earth (27.3 days).

247 A lunar eclipse occurs when the Moon comes between the Sun and the Earth. During the eclipse, the Moon appears to be red in colour. This eclipse generally occurs during a full moon. In ancient times, when people had not understood the reason behind a lunar eclipse, they used to get scared of it. Many superstitions grew as a result of this.

248 Do you know that there is water on the Moon? It seems surprising because the Moon does not have a dense atmosphere, but it is true that there is frozen water that has leaked into shadowed craters and beneath the soil itself. Where did this water come from? It might have come from the solar winds or may have been deposited by comets. However, scientists are not sure there is sufficient ice on the Moon to support human life.

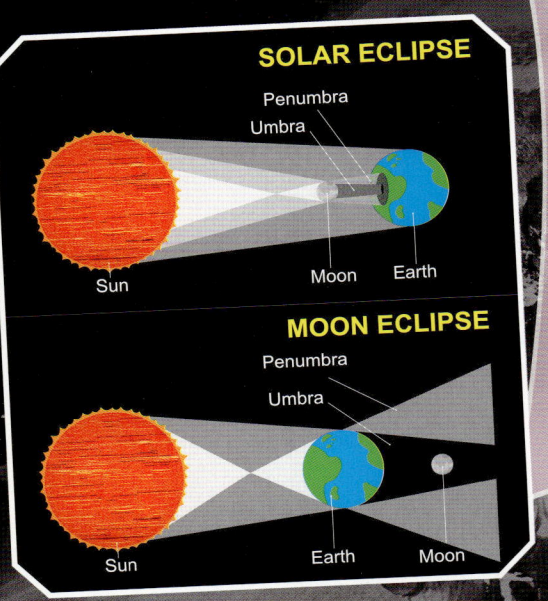

249 Some lunar eclipses can last up to three hours and 45 minutes. Some might even alternate between a solar and a lunar eclipse. Like a solar eclipse, there are three types of lunar eclipses—partial, full and penumbral. In a year, there can be as many as three or four lunar eclipses.

250 A partial lunar eclipse happens when the Earth moves between the Sun and the Moon. However, the three celestial bodies are not aligned in a perfectly straight line. During this, only a portion of the Moon passes through the Earth's shadow. Hence, only a small part of the Moon's surface is covered by the central part of the Earth's shadow.

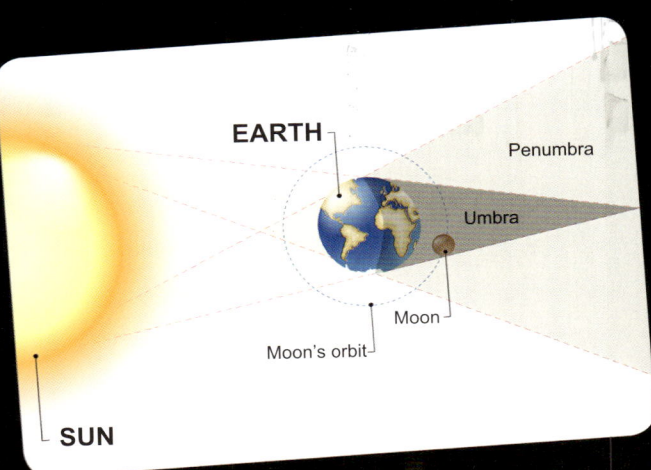

251 In a total or full lunar eclipse, the Sun, Earth and Moon form a straight line. It occurs when the Earth passes directly in front of a full Moon. The Earth itself blocks the sunlight from reaching the Moon. What causes a total lunar eclipse? It occurs when the Sun's light reflects the Earth's shadow on the Moon and the shadow covers the Moon completely.

252 A penumbral lunar eclipse diffuses the outer shadow of Earth which falls on the Moon's face. When the Moon passes through the penumbral shadow of the Earth, this lunar eclipse occurs. This kind of eclipse is very difficult to observe in comparison to total or partial lunar eclipse. According to Fred Espenak, an eclipse expert, almost 35 per cent of lunar eclipses are penumbral.

253 Do you know that the appearance of the Moon seems to change during a total eclipse? It may appear either bright or dull. This is due to variation in the composition of the Earth's atmosphere. A scale is used to denote the darkness of total lunar eclipse known as the Danjon Scale. This scale has five points that range from zero to four.

SOLAR SYSTEM

254 The word 'eclipse' was derived from a Greek word, which means 'downfall'. Sometimes during a full lunar eclipse, the Moon acquires a deep red glow. This is referred to as Blood Moon. This happens only during a total eclipse, that is, when the Sun, the Earth and the Moon are almost in a straight line. The technical term for this is a 'syzygy'. This term came from the Greek word that means 'being paired together'.

255 The average temperature of the surface of the Moon during the day is 107 degree Celsius. At night, it drops to -183 degrees Celsius. As the Moon does not have its own light and only reflects the light of the Sun, it is not harmful to look directly at the Moon. We can observe a lunar eclipse directly with our naked eye, unlike a solar eclipse.

256 The Moon has dust on its surface, which moves and dances! The earliest astronauts who landed on the Moon noticed that at sunrise and sunset, the dust on the Moon seems to move and swirl around. More research was carried out during the LADDE mission. Scientists then came to conclusion that the dust particles seem to move because of an electric charge.

Mars

257 Mars is the second smallest planet in our Solar System, after Mercury. The name Mars is derived from the Roman god of war. The planet is also known by other names. The ancient Greeks called it Ares, the Chinese astronomers called it the 'Fire Star', the Romans associated its blood-red colour with Mars, while the Egyptians called it 'Her Desher' or the 'Red One'.

258 Mars is the fourth planet from the Sun. This planet is red in appearance due to the rock and dust which covers its surface, which is rich in iron. The planet is thus known as the 'Red Planet'. It is a terrestrial planet with a thin layer of atmosphere surrounding it which mainly comprises carbon dioxide (CO_2).

259 Mars has a total mass of 6.42×10^{23} kg (10.7 per cent of Earth). Do you know that Mars experiences the largest dust storms of all the planets in our Solar System? The dust storms can be so severe that they cover the entire planet in a blanket of dust. Its oval-shaped orbital path around the Sun is also the longest. This causes extreme seasonal variations on Mars.

SOLAR SYSTEM

260 After a lot of research, scientists have found tiny particles of Martian atmosphere along with meteorites in our Solar System. They have been orbiting for millions of years now. Some of these particles have also landed on Earth. Scientists have studied these particles to understand and learn more about Mars and its composition.

261 **It is estimated that Mars and Earth have almost the same landmass.** Mars has only 15 and 10 per cent of the Earth's mass and volume. However, since 2/3rd of the Earth is covered with water, the actual landmass of Earth is equivalent to that of Mars. Its surface gravity is just 37 per cent of the Earth. This means we can leap three times higher on Mars.

262 **Do you know that Mars is home to the tallest mountain in our Solar System?** It is called Olympus Mons and is a volcanic mountain, which is 21 kilometres in height and 600 kilometres in diameter. It was formed billions of years ago. The volcano is believed to still be active.

263 Mars was first discovered by Egyptian astronomers in the 2nd millennium BCE. According to their predictions and research, in the coming 20 to 40 million years, Mars will appear to have a ring around it, which will continue to exist for a 100 million years. Phobos, Mars' largest moon is likely to be destroyed, and the debris and dust will add to the formation of this ring.

264 Mars has a surface temperature which varies between -153 degree to 20 degree Celsius. For a long time, it was believed that Mars had water in the form of ice. With the help of satellite images, dark lines of water, and patches on craters and cliffs have clearly been seen. Scientists believe that this water might be salty due to the atmospheric conditions on Mars.

265 Though 40 missions to Mars have been planned, only 18 missions have been successful. The most recent one by NASA was Mars Atmosphere and Volatile Evolution Mission (MAVEN) in 2013. Did you know that India has also successfully managed to send a mission to Mars? This was possible thanks to the work and effort of the team at Indian Space Research Organisation (ISRO). The Indian orbiter was named MOM Mangalyaan and was launched on September 24, 2014. In September 2016, the European Space Agency's ExoMars mission, consisting an orbiter, lander and a rover, was also launched.

SOLAR SYSTEM

266 **From Mars the Sun seems to be about half the size as it seems on Earth.** This is because of its long orbit around the Sun. When Mars' southern hemisphere faces the Sun, it experiences a short, hot summer. On the other hand, when Mars' northern hemisphere faces the Sun, it causes a long and mild summer.

267 **Mars has two moons: Phobos and Deimos.** Of these, Phobos is larger, but it is believed to be decaying. Did you know that we would weigh less on Mars than on Earth? This is because Mars and the Earth differ in size and their gravitational pull is also different. The mass of Mars is 0.017 per cent that of Earth's mass, whereas its gravity is 62 per cent less than that of Earth.

268 **Mars has two permanent ice caps.** According to scientists, layers of dust and ice on Mars are evidence of the changes which occur in its climatic conditions. As seasons change, the ice caps grow and shrink accordingly. The polar ice cap in the north is larger in size, spread across an area of 1,100 kilometres. While both the ice caps are made of ice, they also have a thin layer of frozen carbon dioxide (dry ice).

Jupiter

269 **Jupiter is the fifth planet from the Sun and is the fourth brightest object in our Solar System.** It has an equatorialdiameter of 142,984 kilometres and a polar diameter of 133,709 kilometres. It has the shortest days as compared with all the planets in the Solar System. Jupiter spins very fast on its axis, once every nine hours and 56 minutes.

270 **Do you know that Jupiter has an oblate shape?** It is due to its quick rotation, which has lightly flattened it. It is two-and-a-half times more massive than all the other planets combined. It is mainly made up of gas, and that is why it is sometimes also known as a 'Gas Giant'.

271 **Jupiter is made up of rock, metal and hydrogen compounds.** Its atmosphere contains 90 per cent hydrogen and the remaining 10 per cent is made up of helium and small traces of other gases. As there is no solid ground, its surface is a point where the level of atmospheric pressure is equivalent to that of the Earth.

SOLAR SYSTEM

272 The earliest records of Jupiter can be traced back to the 7th–8th century BCE Babylonians. Like the other planets, Jupiter has also been known by many different names. Jupiter was the name of the head of the Roman gods. For the Greeks, it symbolised Zeus, the God of thunder, while the Mesopotamians called it after Marduk, the patron of the city of Babylon.

273 Jupiter, just like Venus, is visible to the naked eye from Earth. Do you know that its uppermost atmosphere is divided into cloud belts and zones? Its atmosphere is largely made up of ammonia, sulphur, and a mixture of the two compounds.

274 Jupiter has a total mass of 1.90×10^{27} kilograms (which is equal to 318 Earths). It has four rings. It has a longer orbit than the Earth, and moves around the Sun once every 11.8 years. From the point of view of Earth, it moves very slowly across the sky and can take months to pass from one constellation to another.

JUPITER

275 The Great Red Spot is a huge, spinning storm on Jupiter. It is like the hurricanes we see on Earth. However, it is so large that three Earths could fit into it! The wind which moves inside the storm has a speed of about 270 miles per hour. This spot is the most noticeable feature on the Jupiter's surface.

276 Jupiter has more than 50 Moons. These moons are also known as the Jovian Satellites. Do you know which is Jupiter's largest moon? It is Ganymede, which measures 5,268 kilometres across. This moon is larger than Mercury. Ganymede was discovered in 1610 by the astronomer Galileo Galilei.

277 Do you know that Jupiter has a very thin ring system? The rings are mostly made up of dust particles left behind from the collision of comets and asteroids on the surface of the planet. Jupiter's rings start from 92,000 kilometres above the planet and spread over an area of more than 225,000 kilometres from the planet. The four rings are 2,000 to 12,500 kilometres wide.

SOLAR SYSTEM

278 **Europa is the sixth largest moon in the Solar System.** The name Europa is derived from a character in Greek mythology. This moon was also discovered by Galileo Galilei in 1610, and was the smallest of the four Jovian Satellites he had discovered. The size of this moon is just about equivalent to size of Earth's Moon. Europa moves around Jupiter in a circular orbit.

279 **Do you know how many space crafts have gone to Jupiter so far?** As many as eight space crafts have visited this planet. These are: Pioneer 10 and 11, Voyager 1 and 2, Galileo, Cassini, Ulysses, and New Horizons. The most recent spacecraft which landed on Jupiter was in July 2016, and was called the Juno Mission. The upcoming missions will most likely focus on the Jovian moons - Europa, Ganymede and Callisto, and their subsurface oceans.

280 **Jupiter's second-largest moon is Callisto.** It is the closest moon to the planet, and its size is almost the same as that of Mercury. It was discovered by Galileo Galilei in 1610. Its main feature is its multi-ringed impact basin known as Valhalla. It has the largest numbers of craters on its surface.

Saturn

281 **Saturn is the second largest planet, and the sixth planet from the Sun.** It is most well-known for its amazing ring system which was first noticed by the astronomer Galileo Galilei. It is one of the four gas giants in our Solar System. These gas giants or planets are also known as the Jovian Planets.

282 **Have you ever wondered what Saturn is made up of?** It is composed of a mixture of gases, like hydrogen and helium. It has a mean density of 0.687 g/cm3. This means it has a density even lower than water! Though scientists believe the planet has a solid core, it doesn't have a definite solid surface.

283 **Do you know that Saturn is the fifth object in our Solar System which can be seen clearly using just a small telescope?** It was first recorded by Assyrians in the 8th century BCE. It was given the nickname 'Lubadsagush' by them, which means 'oldest of the old'. Its present name comes from the Roman god, Saturnus. The Greeks called it Cronus.

SOLAR SYSTEM

284 **Saturn is the flattest planet of the Solar System.** It spins so quickly on its axis that it flattens itself out at the poles, causing the equator to bulge out even more. It moves on its axis once every 10 hours and 34 minutes. It thus experiences the second shortest day in our Solar System, after Jupiter.

285 **Saturn's outer atmosphere is constituted of about 96.3 per cent hydrogen and 3.25 per cent helium.** It also contains some heavier elements whose proportions are not known. Scientists believe that deep inside the planet, hydrogen becomes metallic. In the areas surrounding the planet, some traces of ammonia, acetylene, ethane, propane, phosphate and methane have also been detected. The upper layers of the clouds contain ammonia ice crystals and below it, the clouds have ice water.

286 **Saturn has a total mass of 5.68×10^{26} kg (equivalent to 95 Earths).** It has an equatorial diameter of 120536 kilometres and a polar diameter of 108,728 kilometres. Its atmosphere also exhibits the same banded pattern like Jupiter, but Saturn's bands are wider near the Equator.

SATURN

287 Do you know that Saturn has the same oval-shaped storms like Jupiter? On Jupiter, this has caused the formation of the Great Red Spot, whereas on Saturn we can observe the Great White Spot. This is a unique and short phenomenon which occurs once in every Saturnian year. Approximately every 30 Earth years, around the time of the northern hemisphere's summer solstice, these storms can be observed. These spots are very wide and were noticed in 1876, 1903, 1933, 1960 and 1990.

288 Saturn's orbital distance, or the time it takes to go around the Sun is 10,756 days (29.5 Earth years). Another interesting fact is that in 2010, a huge band of white clouds known as the Northern Electrostatic Disturbance was noticed by the Cassini space probe. According to the predictions made by scientists, if the periodic nature of storms continues, the next major storm will occur in 2020.

289 Saturn is best known for its extensive ring system. The age of the rings that surround it remains a mystery. They are made of pieces of ice and small amounts of carbonaceous dust. These rings are believed to have been around for about 4.54 billion years. They spread for a distance of 120,700 kilometres from the planet, but are very thin, at around 20 metres wide.

GASEOUS ATMOSPHERE
MOLECULAR HYDROGEN
METALLIC HYDROGEN
ICE
ROCK

SATURN **RADIATES HEAT** INTO SPACE TWO TIMES MORE THAN IT RECEIVES FROM THE SUN

MORE THAN **40% OF THE SATELLITES** OF THE SOLAR SYSTEM REVOLVES AROUND SATURN

SOLAR SYSTEM

290 Do you know that so far only four spacecrafts have gone to Saturn? Of these three were just brief flybys. The first was Pioneer 11 in 1979. The next one was Voyager 1 in 1980 and then Voyager 2 in 1981. Finally, the fourth and most recent one was the Cassini-Huygens mission which continues to move around Saturn and send back photographs of the planet, its moons and rings.

291 Saturn has around 67 discovered moons. All the moons are different in size. Titan, one its moons, is the second largest moon in our Solar System. It has a wide and nitrogen rich atmosphere and is composed mainly of water, ice and rock. Most of Saturn's moons are very small, just a few kilometres around, and have no official names.

292 Do you know that sometimes the rings of Saturn disappear? In fact, they do not exactly disappear, but appear to move away. As Saturn is tilted like Earth, it keeps changing its position around the Sun every 30 years. This is why sometimes the rings are fully visible, while other times they are on the edge and seem to disappear. This occurred in 2008–2009 and the next such phenomenon is predicted in 2024–2025.

Uranus

293

Uranus is the seventh planet from the Sun, and is double the distance from the Sun as compared to Saturn. For us, it is not possible to see Uranus with the naked eye. It was the first planet which was discovered with the help of the telescope. Can you imagine, just by the discovery of Uranus, the size of the Solar System actually doubled!

294

Sir William Herschel was the person who discovered Uranus in 1781. Initially, Herschel thought that it was a comet, but after some years of observation he realised that it was a planet. He wanted to name this planet 'Georgian Sidus', but another astronomer Johann Bode gave it the name Uranus. The name comes from the ancient Greek deity Ouranos.

295

Uranus has a total mass of 8.68×10^{25} kg (equivalent to 15 Earths). It has an equatorial diameter of 51,118 kilometres and polar diameter of 49,946 kilometres.

SOLAR SYSTEM

296

Do you know that Uranus records the lowest temperatures in the Solar System? Uranus has minimum atmospheric pressure of -224 degree Celsius. It has an average temperature of -197 degree Celsius at the cloud tops but can go as low as -226 degree Celsius. It is a gas giant, and has an atmosphere composed of methane ice crystals, water and ammonia. The planet itself is largely composed of Hydrogen and helium.

297
Uranus experiences very powerful winds which can reach up to 250 metres per second. It generates anticyclone storms. Due to presence of methane in its atmosphere, the planet has a light aquamarine colour. There are also some traces of hydrocarbons like ethane, acetylene, methylacetylene, and diacetelyne which interact with solar ultraviolent radiation.

SOLAR SYSTEM
URANUS

298
The core of Uranus is composed of rock and ice. The planet also contains traces of water, ammonia, carbon dioxide, carbon monoxide, and hydrogen sulphide. Because of the cold, they are released in an icy state and hence the planet is known as an ice giant.

URANUS

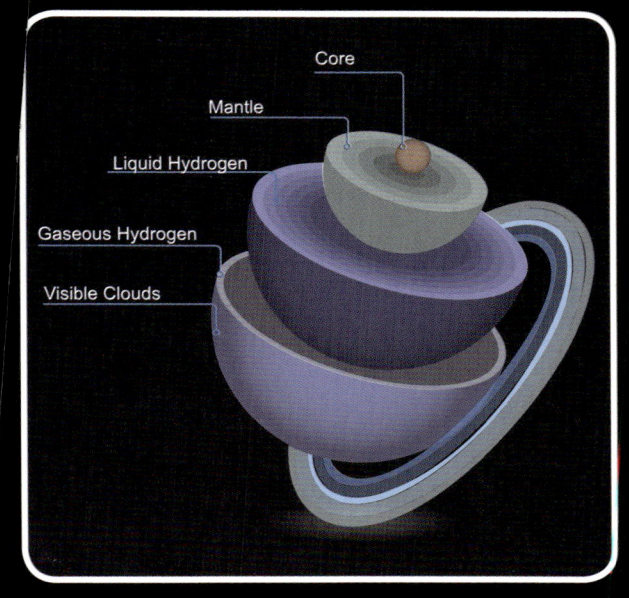

299 Do you know that Uranus is the second least dense planet in our Solar System, after Saturn? We know that Uranus is 14.5 times as massive as the Earth. It has a mean density of 1.27 g/cm3. There is an interesting side effect of its low density—we would experience only about 89 per cent of gravitational force at the Uranus cloud tops!

300 How many rings does Uranus have? It has two sets of rings which are dark in colour. They are made up of small, dark particles of different sizes. Currently, scientists have discovered 13 rings, of which 11 are inner rings and two are outer rings. Among these, the brightest is the Epsilon ring. The rings were first discovered in 1977 by James Elliot, Douglas Mink and Edward Dunham.

301 Uranus has 27 moons, which are small and irregular in shape. The largest moons of Uranus are, in order of size, Miranda, Ariel, Umbriel, Oberon and Titania. While Miranda, Ariel, Oberon and Titania get their names from characters in William Shakespeare's plays, Umbriel gets its name form a famous poem by Alexander Pope.

302 Till now only one spacecraft has gone to Uranus. The spacecraft Voyager 2 reached the planet on January 24, 1986. The probe flew past Uranus from a distance of approximately 81,500 km. It brought back close-up images of the planet, its moons and rings. No other spacecraft has ever been sent after this, and astronomers don't have any current plans to send more probes to Uranus.

303 The planet is sharply tilted, possibly due to a collision many years ago. It now has an axial tilt of 98 degree. This is why one of its poles always faces the Sun. Thus, at the North Pole a day lasts for half of its year, which is the same as 84 Earth years. One season thus lasts for around 42 years on Uranus.

304

Did you know that a day on Uranus lasts for about 17 hours and 14 minutes? It is also the only other planet apart from Venus, which spins in a retrograde direction on its axis.

Neptune

305 **Neptune is the eighth planet from the Sun.** Scientists believe that before migrating to its current position, in the early phase of the Solar System this planet may have been formed much closer to the Sun. It is last of the known planets. While it is the third largest planet in respect to mass, it is only the fourth largest in terms of diameter.

306 **Neptune is a gas giant, and was named after the Roman god of the sea due to its blue colour.** It was not known to the ancients as it cannot be seen with the naked eye. It was first noticed in 1846 and astronomers fixed its position with the help of mathematical predictions.

307 **Neptune spins very quickly on its axis.** The planet's equatorial clouds take just 18 hours to make one rotation. This is because Neptune is not a solid body. It takes Neptune 164.8 Earth years to orbit around the Sun. On July 11, 2001, it completed its first full orbit after it was discovered in 1846!

SOLAR SYSTEM

308 **Do you know who discovered the planet Neptune?** It was discovered on September 23, 1846 by Jean Joseph Le Verrier. This planet was not previously known and was thus initially named Le Verrier after its discoverer. Later on, this name was replaced by 'Neptune'.

309 **Neptune is the smallest of the ice giants.** Though smaller than Uranus, Neptune has a greater mass. Its inner core is made of rock. The atmosphere is made of hydrogen and helium with some amount of methane. The methane absorbs red light and makes the planet appear bluish.

310 **A lot of activity has been observed in Neptune's atmosphere.** Large storms seem to take place in its upper atmosphere, and high winds with speeds of up to 1,340 kilometres per second blow around the planet.

311 **Neptune has a well-organised ring system.** It has a thin, faint collection of rings. They are primarily made up of ice particles mixed with dust granules, coated with a carbon-based substance. The atmosphere of Neptune is divided into the lower troposphere and the stratosphere, with the tropopause being the boundary between the two spheres.

312 **Astronomers have discovered 14 moons of Neptune.** The largest Neptunian moon, Triton, was discovered just 17 days after Neptune itself was discovered. It is a frozen world, composed of water-ice crust and frozen nitrogen over a core of rock and metal core. Triton orbits the planet in a retrograde orbit, which makes scientists suggest that it was a dwarf planet captured by Neptune's gravitational pull.

VOYAGER
Neptune

313
So far, only one spacecraft has flown by Neptune. In 1989, the Voyager 2 spacecraft flew past the planet and captured the first close up pictures of the Neptunian system. It took about 246 minutes—four hours and six minutes—for the signals from Voyager 2 to return to Earth. The NASA/ESA Hubble Space Telescope has also studied the planet.

314 **Do you know about Neptune's Great Dark Spot?** It was found in the southern part of the planet by Voyager 2 in 1989. It was formed due to a large rotating storm system, with winds up to 1,500 miles per hour. These were the strongest winds ever recorded on any planet. Neptune has also got a second storm, known as the Small Dark Spot. This storm is almost the same size as the Earth's moon. This spot is similar to the Great Red Spot seen on Jupiter.

SOLAR SYSTEM

315 An interesting fact about Neptune is that its orbital path is approximately 30 astronomical units (AU) from the Sun. It means that its distance is 30 times the distance from the Earth to the Sun.

NEPTUNE

DISTANCE FROM THE SUN: 4.498E9 km
RADIUS: 1737 km
SURFACE AREA: 7.618E9 km2
DAY LENGTH: 0d 16h 6min
ORBITAL PERIOD: 165 years
SURFACE TEMPERATURE: -231°C
MOONS: 14

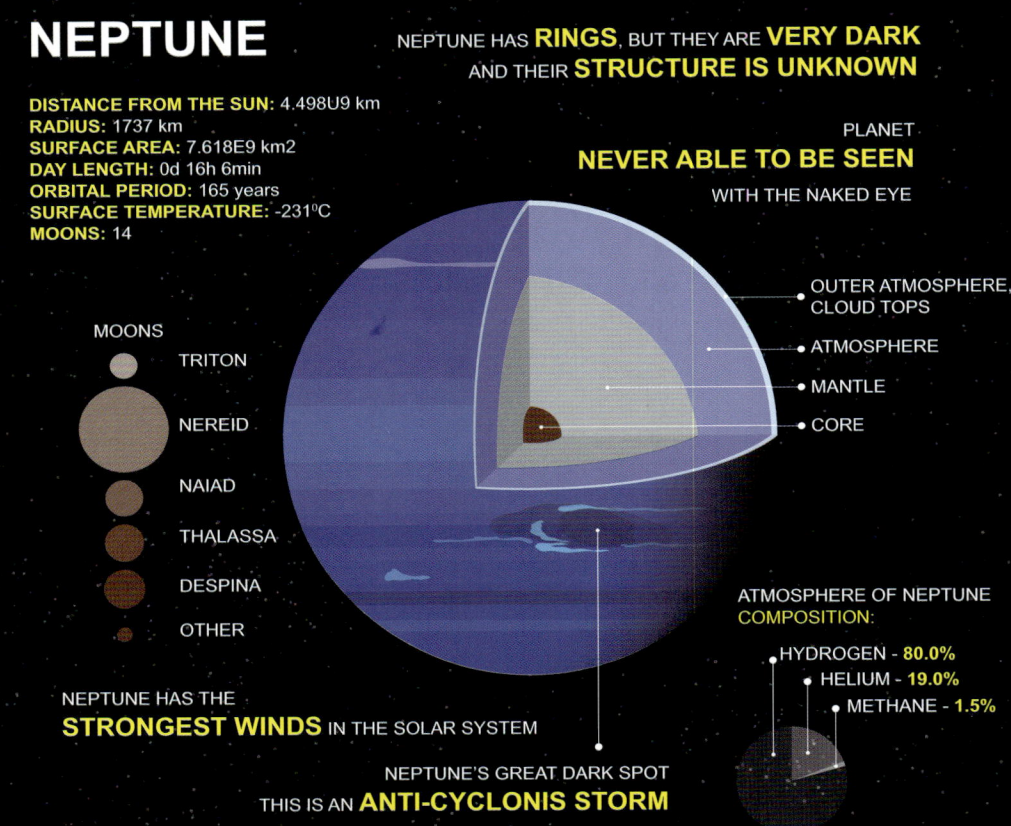

NEPTUNE HAS **RINGS**, BUT THEY ARE **VERY DARK** AND THEIR **STRUCTURE IS UNKNOWN**

PLANET **NEVER ABLE TO BE SEEN** WITH THE NAKED EYE

- OUTER ATMOSPHERE, CLOUD TOPS
- ATMOSPHERE
- MANTLE
- CORE

MOONS
- TRITON
- NEREID
- NAIAD
- THALASSA
- DESPINA
- OTHER

NEPTUNE HAS THE **STRONGEST WINDS** IN THE SOLAR SYSTEM

NEPTUNE'S GREAT DARK SPOT THIS IS AN **ANTI-CYCLONIS STORM**

ATMOSPHERE OF NEPTUNE COMPOSITION:
- HYDROGEN - **80.0%**
- HELIUM - **19.0%**
- METHANE - **1.5%**

316 The interior of Neptune is somewhat similar to that of Uranus. It is made of two layers—a core and mantle. The core is rocky and almost 1.2 times as massive as the Earth. The mantle is an extremely very hot and dense fluid composed of water, ammonia and methane. The mantle is 10 to 15 times the mass of the Earth.

Pluto

317 **Pluto was once considered the ninth and most distant planet from the Sun.** It takes Pluto 246.04 Earth years to orbit the Sun. It was discovered in 1930 and continued to be considered a planet until 2006. Pluto is a member of the Kuiper Belt.

318 **Do you know how Pluto got its name?** It was named after the Greek God of the underworld, the Roman alternative for the Greek God Hades. The name was proposed by Venetia Burney, an 11-year-old schoolgirl from Oxford, England.

319 **In 2006, Pluto was reclassified from a planet to a dwarf planet.** This happened after the IAU formalised the definition of a planet as follows: "A planet is a celestial body that (a) is in orbit around the Sun, (b) has sufficient mass for its self-gravity to overcome rigid body forces so that it assumes a hydrostatic equilibrium (nearly round) shape, and (c) has cleared the neighbourhood around its orbit."

320 **It was discovered on 18 February 1930 by Clyde Tombaugh of the Lowell Observatory.** In the 76 years between the period of its discovery and subsequent reclassification as a dwarf planet, Pluto has only completed less than one-third of its orbit around the Sun!

SOLAR SYSTEM

321 **Do you know that Pluto is even smaller than some of the moons in the Solar System?** For instance, Ganymede, Titan, Callisto, Io, Europa, Triton and the Earth's Moon are all larger than Pluto. It has 66 per cent of the diameter of the Earth's Moon and 18 per cent of its mass. When it was discovered, its small size actually surprised the scientists who had first assumed that it would be as large as Jupiter!

322 **When Pluto comes closer to the Sun on its elliptical orbital path, the surface ice thaws and results in the formation of a thin atmosphere of nitrogen, methane and carbon monoxide.** Nitrogen is present in large amounts, along with methane, which covers an area of 161 km above the surface. However, when Pluto travels further away from the Sun, the gases once again freeze back into the solid state.

323 **Do you know Pluto does not have a simple circular orbit?** It has an eccentric and inclined orbit which takes it in between 4.4 and 7.3 billion km from the Sun. This actually means that at some points, it is closer to the Sun than Neptune. In fact, its orbit actually led to its discovery. Pluto's location was predicted in 1915 by Percival Lowell. This prediction was based on the deviations which he had observed in 1905 in the orbits of Uranus and Neptune.

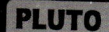

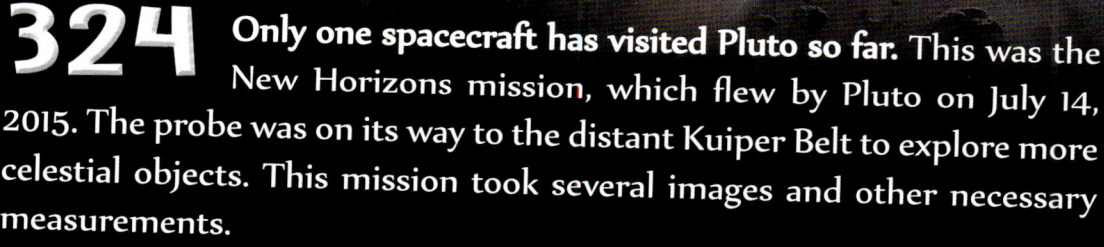

324 **Only one spacecraft has visited Pluto so far.** This was the New Horizons mission, which flew by Pluto on July 14, 2015. The probe was on its way to the distant Kuiper Belt to explore more celestial objects. This mission took several images and other necessary measurements.

325 **Do you know if the surface of Pluto has any water?** In fact, the planet is composed of one-third water, which is in the form of ice; this is more than four times the water present in all the Earth's oceans. The other two-thirds part of Pluto is formed of rock. Its surface has different mountain ranges, light and dark areas and scattered craters. It is covered with a water ice mantle and a frozen nitrogen surface.

326 **Pluto has a total mass of 1.31×10^{22} kg. It has five known moons:** Charon, which was discovered in 1978; Hydra and Nix, both found in 2005; Kerberous (originally P4) discovered in 2011; and Styx (originally P5) found in 2012. Do you know that Pluto and its moon Charon form a binary system? This means that the centre of mass of two objects is outside of it. Pluto moves in small circles and Charon orbits it.

SOLAR SYSTEM

327 **Pluto is the largest dwarf planet in the Solar System.** At one point, it was believed that Eris was the largest dwarf planet. According to recent accurate measurements, Eris has an average diameter of 2,326 kilometres with a margin of error of 12 kilometres, while Pluto has a diameter of 2,372 kilometres with a two-kilometre margin of error. It is predicted that Pluto's core forms around 70 per cent of its total diameter.

328 **Have you heard the term 'Plutoid'?** This term is used to describe objects in our Solar System that are round and orbit the Sun beyond the orbit of Neptune. At present, there are four recognised Plutoids: Pluto, Eris, Haumea and Makemake. According to astronomers, they are probably at least 70 more such celestial objects that may be classified as Plutoids.

Asteroids

329 Asteroids are small, airless, rocky celestial bodies which keep on revolving around the Sun and different planets. They are so small in size that they cannot be called planets. Instead, they are known as planetoids or minor planets. There are millions of asteroids in the Solar System, and they are often grouped together according to their composition.

330 Do you know that the total mass of all the asteroids is less than that of the Earth's Moon? However, despite their small size, they can be dangerous. Many asteroids have hit the Earth in the past and it is quite likely that more could collide with our planet in the near future. This is why scientists try to learn more about their number, orbits, and physical characteristics.

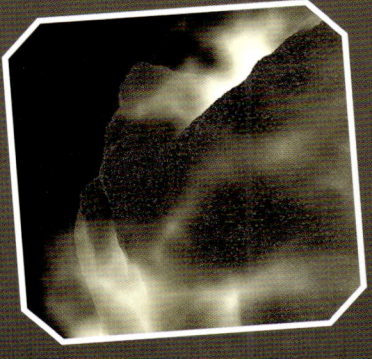

331 Have you ever wondered how these asteroids were formed? They are made of materials left over from the formation of the inner Solar System. It is also believed that when small celestial objects collided with each other, they fragmented, giving birth to asteroids. Asteroids are all of different sizes and shapes. For instance, some are as large as Ceres, 940 kilometres across, while others are only about 20 feet across.

332 Asteroids have been found to be of three main kinds— the C-types (chondrites), S-types and M-types. These categories denote how far from the Sun they were formed in the early period of the Solar System. C-types are made of water, metal and organic compounds, S-types are made of clay and silicate rocks, while M-types are made of metallic nickel-iron.

SOLAR SYSTEM

333 Do you know that most of asteroids are found in between the orbits of Mars and Jupiter? This is known as the Asteroid Belt. Apart from these, there are a number of near-Earth asteroids known as Athens, Amors and Apollos. These lie near or on the Earth's orbital path. Similarly, a number of asteroids called Trojans lie along Jupiter's orbital path.

334 Do you know that some asteroids have their own moons? Most asteroids have irregular shapes, while very few are spherical. They are also usually rich in precious metals and other metals, as well as water. It is believed that the surface of most asteroids is covered with dust.

335 Asteroids that come very close to the path of the Earth are known as near-Earth objects (NEOs) or Potentially Hazardous Asteroids (PHAs). The amount of harm caused by asteroids in our atmosphere depends on the size of the object. When small asteroids enter the Earth's atmosphere, they are known as meteors and meteorites. Scientists often study these NEOs in order to predict and study the possible collisions with the asteroids.

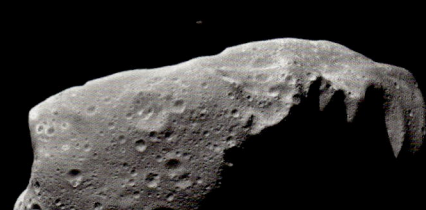

ASTEROIDS

336 **The most famous asteroids are Ceres, Pallas and Vesta.** These are rocky minor planets, and have been observed by astronomers since the 1800s. Ceres is 945 kilometres across. It was thought to be a differentiated asteroid, but now it is considered a dwarf planet. Pallas has a very non-uniform shape with a diameter of 512 kilometres. Vesta is very bright, and is left over from a rocky proto-planet. It measures about 580 kilometres across.

337 **As we all know, asteroids are very small in comparison to planets.** Thus, they cannot support life. Due to their size, they cannot even hold onto an atmosphere. They usually have irregular shapes, as their gravity is too weak to pull their shape into a circle. According to NASA, they have a tenuous exosphere.

338 **Do you know that scientists have found evidence that water may flow on asteroids?** In 2015, it was found that Vesta has gullies that may have been formed by the flow of water. When a smaller asteroid collides with a bigger one, material gets transferred from one to the other. Heat from the impact would melt the ice on the asteroid surfaces, causing it to flow across the surface.

Comets

339 Comets are very small bodies made of ice with a small amount of rock and minerals. Comets mainly contain a solid nucleus which is covered with a cloud of ice and dust. It is surrounded with a gas known as coma. The nucleus contains frozen water, rock, methane, nitrogen and carbon. It has also been called a dirty snowball.

340 Comets have their own atmosphere. The gas which emerges from the nucleus forms a thin atmosphere that can reach up to 60,000 miles in diameter. In 2007, the coma of the Comet Holmes was measure to be 869,900 miles in diameter. This was even larger than the diameter of the Sun!

341 **All comets orbit the Sun.** Perihelion is the point in the orbit of a comet when it is closest to the sun. Aphelion is the farthest point of its orbit. The shapes and sizes of all comets are different. As the comets come closer to the Sun, they start reacting to the heat. This causes some of the ice to sublimate. If the ice is close to the outer surface of the comet, it may emerge from it like a mini-geyser.

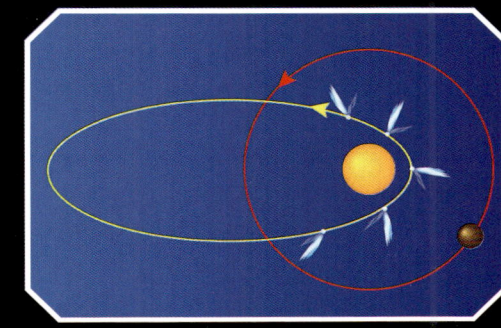

342 **Several long-period comets actually emerge from the Oort Cloud.** This is a cloud of cosmic material that is located millions of times farther than the Kuiper Belt. These types of comets can take millions of years to complete their orbit. Short-period comets usually come from the Kuiper Belt situated beyond Neptune's orbit, and usually take less than 200 years to complete an orbit.

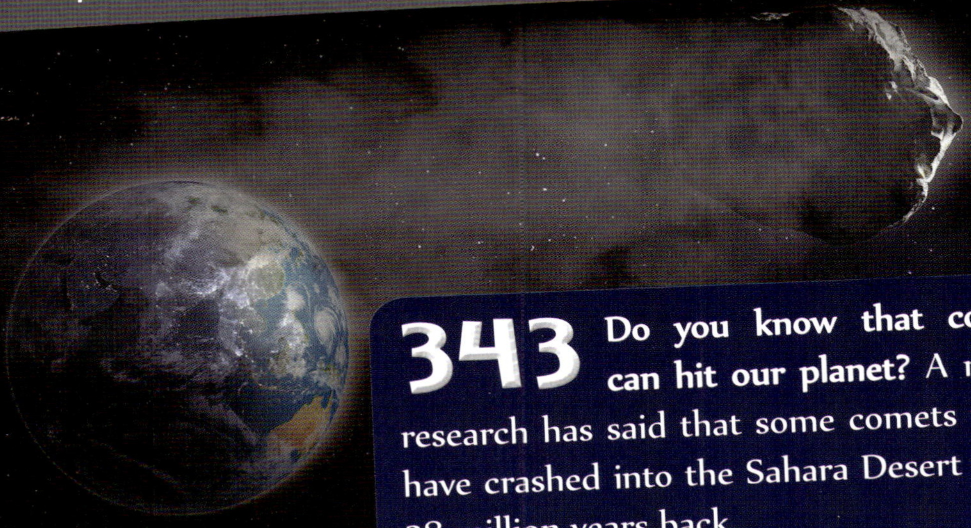

343 **Do you know that comets can hit our planet?** A recent research has said that some comets might have crashed into the Sahara Desert about 28 million years back.

SOLAR SYSTEM

344 **When the comet nears the Sun, the coma stretches out behind the comet in a long tail.** Usually comets have two tails. Of these, one is a dust tail which is easily visible with the naked eye. The other is a plasma tail, made up of gases, which glow on ionisation.

345 **Comets have elliptical orbits in which they move around the Sun.** Some comets take millions of years to complete their orbit while some take short periods, for example: the Halley's Comet, takes 76 years to complete its orbit. Sometimes comets also break up if they come too close to the Sun or a planet in orbit.

346 **Some of the comets do not go very close to the Sun, while some get so close that they break into tiny pieces.** Such comets are known as sungrazers. Once, comets were even known as 'hairy stars'.

347 **The interesting thing about comet Hale-Bopp is that it can be seen from Earth for 18 months.** The tail of the comet is formed due to the heat of sun which evaporates ice into gas and increases the size of the comet's coma. Sometimes, if the Earth happens to pass through the stream of the comet's orbit, material from the comet's tail falls to the Earth, creating meteor showers.

348 **Comets are of two types: Periodic and non-periodic.** Some most famous comets are non-periodic comets like Hale-Bopp (C/1995 O1), Hyakutake (C/1996 B2), McNaught (C2006 P1), and Lovejoy (C/2011 W3). The periodic comet Halley is the most well-known comet in history. It returns to the inner Solar System once every 76 years. Another famous comet is 2P/Encke which appears every 3.3 years.

Meteors

349 The small pieces of rock, dust and metal entering the Earth's atmosphere are known as meteors. Some meteors are part of asteroids or small pieces of debris from Mars, the Moon or comets. Most meteors burn up within seconds of entering the atmosphere, but some larger meteors survive and fall on the Earth. These are known as meteorites.

350 Our Solar System is made up of many heavenly bodies, including millions of small meteoroids. Meteoroids which are very small in size are known as space dust or micro-meteoroids. Sometimes small meteoroids pass through the upper atmosphere, creating streaks of light as they burn up due to friction.

351 Millions of meteoroids travel through the Earth's atmosphere each and every day. However, they are usually very small and burn up quickly. Do you know what a meteor shower is? The appearance of a number of meteors in the same area of the sky over a definite period of time is known as a meteor shower.

352 Asteroids sometimes break up to form meteoroids that fall on the Earth. Scientist have classified meteors according to their chemical makeup, isotopic composition and their mineralogy. Beyond this classification, Meteorites are of three types: stony, metallic and mixtures. Stony are made up of rocky material, metallic may contain iron and other metals, while mixtures are stony-irons. These compositions tell us where the meteoroid existed in its parent body.

METEORS

353 **Do you know that when meteors or comets hit the Earth, they leave an impact crater on the Earth's surface?** Due to the high speed with which they travel, the crater is usually much bigger than the body that crashed on the ground. For instance, the crater in the state of Arizona in the US was formed 50,000 years ago. It is 1200 metres in diameter, 170 metres deep, and surrounded by a 45-metre rim, but the asteroid that caused the crater was only about 40 metres wide!

354 **Falling meteors create a streak of light in the sky, and are also known as shooting stars.** The largest meteorite so far has been found in Hoba, West Namibia, which weighed more than 60 tonnes. Other famous meteorites are the Allende Meteorite and the Willamette Meteorite.

355 **The Perseids in August and the Geminids in December are the two big meteors showers which occur every year.** They are caused by debris shed by asteroids. Sometimes meteors also produce sound known as sonic boom. It is a sound heard after the meteors become visible. The Quadrantids are caused by debris from the minor planet 2003 EH1.

SOLAR SYSTEM

356 **Do you know that meteors are visible to us when they are approximately 120 kilometres above the Earth?** Most meteors fall into the ocean, because such a large part of the Earth's surface is covered with water. It is estimated that there are around 9 meteors showers every year. Some occur during the day, when the sunlight makes it impossible to see them.

357 **Sometimes meteors appear to have red, yellow and green tails.** Such colours are caused by the ionization of molecules. For example, if nickel is present in the meteor, the tail will appear to be green.

358 **Do you know the best time to view a meteor shower?** It is during the early morning hours, or on a dark, moonless night. The Orionid Meteor shower which occurs in October in every year is created by dust and debris left behind by the passage of Comet 1P/Halley. The Perseids Meteor shower was first recorded by the Chinese in about 36CE.

ASTRONOMY

Study of Astronomy

359 Astronomy is the study of the celestial bodies like stars, planets and comets, as well as the different phenomena which take place in outer space. People have been trying to study the Universe since prehistoric times in different ways, and Astronomy is sometimes called the oldest natural science.

360 Over the years, Astronomy has been closely associated with other studies, like Astrology and Mathematics. Modern Astronomy involves observation of stars, planets and other observable phenomena. It also uses the other sciences, like Physics and Chemistry, to study the Universe. This has helped scientists learn about the expansion of the Universe, composition of the Sun and other stars, and even the distance between different galaxies.

361 A constellation is made up of a group of stars. Each star of a constellation is named after the Greek alphabet. The brightest star in the constellation is said to be the Alpha star, the next brightest star is called the Beta star, and so on.

ASTRONOMY

362 **Stars are actually several light years away from us.** A light year is the distance travelled by light in the duration of one year. Thus, when we look at the stars from the Earth, we are actually looking into the past. We see the stars as they were several years before, and not as they are at present.

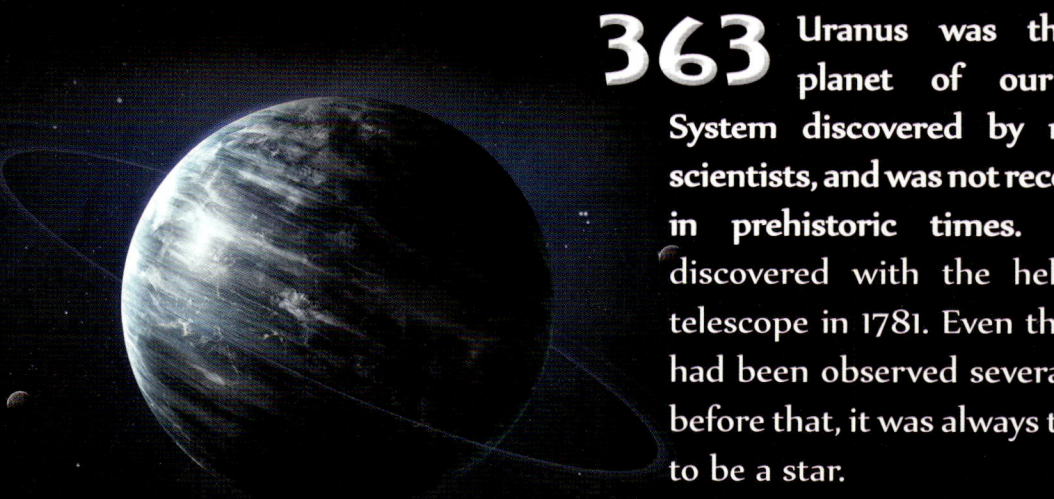

363 **Uranus was the first planet of our Solar System discovered by modern scientists, and was not recognised in prehistoric times.** It was discovered with the help of a telescope in 1781. Even though it had been observed several times before that, it was always thought to be a star.

364 **Mars is also known as the Red Planet due to its red colour.** It is interesting to note that the red colour comes from the rusted or oxidised iron that is present in its soil. On the other hand, Uranus has an atmosphere that absorbs red wavelengths of sunlight. Thus, it appears to be a bluish-green in colour.

STUDY OF ASTRONOMY

365 An object in a Solar System, which is neither a planet nor a natural satellite but has a planetary mass, is known as a dwarf planet. Dwarf planets are in the direct orbit of the Sun and have enough mass to generate their own gravity. There are more than 200 dwarf planets in the region of the Kuiper Belt. Pluto, which was once considered to be the ninth planet of our Solar System, is now labelled as a dwarf planet.

366 In addition to the planets in our Solar System, there exist many other such star systems and planets. The planetary bodies that are not in our Solar System and orbit a star other than the Sun are called extrasolar planets or exoplanets. It was in the year 1992 that the first extrasolar planets were discovered.

367 The brightest star in our night sky is Sirius. It is also known as the Dog Star. It is said to be bigger, brighter and hotter than the Sun. After the Sun, Sirius is the brightest star visible to people on the Earth. It is also easily visible in the sky from most of the northern hemisphere.

ASTRONOMY

368 Between the orbits of planets Jupiter and Neptune, there are several small bodies, with mass similar to the asteroids, and composition similar to comets. They also revolve around the Sun and are called centaur objects.

369 The icy objects that exist in the outer part of the Solar System are surrounded by an extended shell of clouds. Those clouds are known as Oort Clouds. They were named after the Dutch astronomer Jan Oort who was the first to theorise their existence.

370 The Kuiper Belt is a region of space filled with icy bodies, located beyond the planet Neptune. This belt holds trillions of objects including the remnants of the early Solar System. It should not be confused with the Oort cloud that is thousand times more distant than the Kuiper Belt.

STUDY OF ASTRONOMY

371 **The Sun is a star, and is the centre of our Solar System.** The planets and other heavenly bodies revolve around the Sun due to its magnetic field and gravitational pull. In many religions, ancient and modern, Sun is considered to be the most powerful source of life that gives warmth and illumination to humankind.

372 **The innermost planet of our Solar System is Mercury, which is closest to the Sun.** Its existence was known for over 5,000 years. It was also called Apollo in Greek mythology, denoting the god of music, Sun, light, and knowledge. Mercury is the smallest planet of the Solar System.

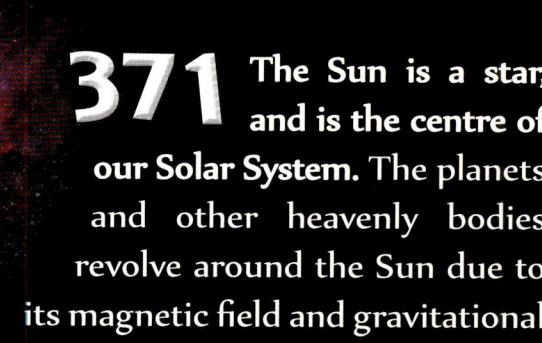

373 **Venus is the closest planet to Earth.** Because of its similar size, mass, and density, it is regarded as Earth's twin. However, the clouds enveloping Venus make it difficult to get a clear picture of its surface and atmosphere. It can also be seen clearly by the naked eye around sunrise or sunset as a bright star.

ASTRONOMY

374 **The Earth is the most outstanding planet in the Solar System.** It is the only planet that is known to support life. Its name is derived from Old English and German words which mean 'ground'. It is the only planet whose name was not derived from the Greco-Roman mythology. Earth consists of about 71 per cent water. The oceans contain about 96.5 per cent of all Earth's water.

375 **Mars is the second closest planet to Earth, after Venus.** Several years of observations have revealed that Mars is somewhat similar to Earth. It has clouds, winds, volcanoes, canyons, and seasonal weather patterns along with other similarities. It is also believed that Mars might have supported life at one time, but it is now a sterile, frozen desert.

376 **An asteroid or planetoid is a mass of rock floating in space.** There is a nearly flat ring of such asteroids between the orbits of Mars and Jupiter, known as the Asteroid Belt. These asteroids also orbit the Sun like the planets. Astronomers also sometimes call them minor planets.

STUDY OF ASTRONOMY

377 **Jupiter is the most massive planet in our Solar System.** It is larger than all the other planets combined. Jupiter has more than 60 known moons. One of those moons, Ganymede, is even bigger than the planet Mercury. Some astronomers have speculated that one of its moons, Europa, may have some kind of life beneath the icy crust of the water present on it.

378 **Saturn is the most glorious planet in the Solar System.** The magnificent rings encircling it give it a unique appearance. Saturn is actually a gas giant because it lacks a definite surface. It may have a solid core, but its atmosphere is predominantly composed of gases such as helium and hydrogen.

379 **Planets can be differentiated on the basis of their composition.** Thus, there are four terrestrial planets and four Jovian or Gas planets in our Solar System. Mercury, Venus, Earth and Mars are the terrestrial planets that are made up of rocks and metals and have a solid surface, while the other four planets have little or no solid surface and are made up of various gases.

ASTRONOMY

380 **Neptune is the smallest amongst the Jovian planets and the atmosphere on the planet is heavily stormy.** Neptune has the fastest winds as compared with any other planet in our Solar System. It was named after the Roman god of sea, who is known as Poseidon in Greek mythology.

381 **Galileo Galilei was an Italian astronomer, physicist, mathematician, and philosopher.** He discovered that Venus also goes through phases just like the Moon. He had also discovered four of the largest satellites of Jupiter, which were named after him. He was the first person to discover the existence of sunspots. Earlier, other scientists had thought that the dark spots on the Sun were its satellites.

382 **Edwin Powell Hubble was an American astronomer who observed that our galaxy is not the only one in the universe.** He also argued that the universe was expanding. The calculation by which this theory was proved came to be known as Hubble's law.

Telescopes

383 The first working telescopes are credited to Hans Lippershey. They were first made in the Netherlands, in 1608. These refracting telescopes were designed with a convex objective lens and a concave eyepiece.

384 Although Lippershey is documented to have patented the telescope, there were many others who claimed to have made the first telescope. Those people included Zacharias Janssen, who was a spectacle-maker, and Jacob Metius, who was an instrument maker specialising in grinding lenses. Both of them lived in the Netherlands.

385 The first working reflector telescope was designed in 1668 and is credited to Isaac Newton. It incorporated a small, flat, diagonal mirror that reflected the light to the eyepiece which was mounted on the side of the telescope.

ASTRONOMY

386 Galileo was the first to use the telescope to study the extra-terrestrial objects in the early 17th century. This was a revolutionary step in the field of astronomy. Before that, magnification instruments had never been used for such purposes. After Galileo's innovative step, more powerful optical telescopes began to develop, improving our ability to study the Universe.

387 Although the telescope was invented in the early 17th century, it was only during the 20th century that more powerful and different kinds of telescopes were developed. These telescopes covered a wide range of wavelengths, from radio to gamma rays.

388 Simple lenses had been made as early as the 2nd century CE. It was in 12th century Europe that 'reading stones' were documented. These referred to magnifying lenses. During the late 13th century and early 14th century, concave and convex lenses were used to correct eyesight. Without these lenses, it would have been impossible to develop telescopes.

389 Initially, telescopes were referred to as the 'Dutch perspective glass', that used to magnify any reading material or make any object appear nearer and larger. It was Galileo's instrument that was the first to be named as a 'telescope'. This word was derived from Greek words that mean 'far-seeing'.

390 Sometimes large areas of the sky have to be seen and photographed for some astronomical applications. It was in 1930 that Bernhard Schmidt invented a telescope that could cover wide areas for observation. It came to be known as the Schmidt telescope and was used for research and survey programmes where a large area of the sky had to be covered, such as searches for asteroids and comets.

391 In 1990, a space telescope named the Hubble Space Telescope (HST) was launched into low orbit around the Earth. It is a man-made satellite. It is one of the largest space telescopes and is still in operation. It is very helpful as a research tool for astronomy. The telescope is one of NASA's great observatories and is named after the astronomer, Edwin Powell Hubble.

ASTRONOMY

392 The Hubble Space Telescope contains a 7.9 - feet mirror and can take extremely high resolutions images outside the Earth's atmosphere. It has taken some of the most detailed images of space, and these have helped scientists to achieve many breakthroughs in astrophysics, including the determination of the expansion of the universe.

393 The United States space agency, National Aeronautics and Space Administration (NASA), had built the Hubble Space Telescope with contributions from the European Space Agency (ESA). The space satellite is controlled by the Goddard Space Flight Centre and the Space Telescope Science Institute (STScI) selects the targets of the telescope and processes the data.

394 The Hubble Space Telescope was first supposed to launch in 1983 but due to some technical delays and budget problems it was finally launched in 1990. After its launch, it was found that the main mirror had been ground incorrectly. Thus, in 1993 a servicing mission went to the telescope to fix its mirror.

TELESCOPES

395 **In California, there is an astronomical observatory located on Mount Wilson, northeast of Los Angeles.** The Mount Wilson Observatory houses two historically important telescopes. One is the Hooker telescope and the other is the Snow Solar telescope.

396 **When the Hooker Telescope was being set up, a 100-inch mirror had to be attached to it.** It took nearly 200 men about eight hours, using ropes and guiding a truck, to complete the long and torturous drive to the top of Mount Wilson, to bring this mirror to the observatory. However, the tiresome work was worth it, as the Hooker telescope helped to prove that there are other galaxies in the Universe and also that the universe is expanding.

397 **Karl Guthe Jansky is considered to be one of the founders of radio astronomy.** Certain telescopes are used to identify radio waves, and not just visible light. In August 1931, Jansky noticed that his equipment was picking up radio sources that were celestial. He later discovered that these radio waves were coming from the Milky Way.

398 One of the weirdest telescopes ever was built by a physicist, Raymond Davis Jr in 1960. Davis used 100,000 gallons of dry-cleaning fluid in order to detect the invisible neutrino particles that were streaming from the Sun. This unique and weird telescope built by Davis actually worked and it revealed fundamental new physics concepts. The telescope won him a Nobel Prize in 2002.

399 Mauna Kea is a sacred site to the Native Hawaiian culture and religion. On the slopes of Mauna Kea 13 telescopes have been set up. In 2015, the Governor of Hawaii, David Y. Ige announced that an 18-storey high Thirty Meter Telescope (TMT) would be constructed on the mountain. This immediately sparked controversy and was opposed by the native public.

400 The European Extremely Large Telescope (E-ELT) is an under construction astronomical observatory. It is targeted to be completed in the year 2024. It will narrowly beat Hawaii's Thirty Meter Telescope to be the world's largest telescope. It will be located on the Cerro Armazones in Chile's Atacama Desert and will have a 128 feet high light-collecting surface.

401 Galileo's 'Sidereus Nuncius' or the 'Starry Messenger' was the first published scientific work based on telescopic observations. It was published in 1610 and was written in New Latin. It offers a detailed view of Galileo's observations of the Moon and hundreds of previously unobserved stars. It also discussed the 'Medicean Stars of Jupiter', as Galileo referred to the moons of Jupiter. The work contains more than 70 drawings and diagrams of the Moon and constellations.

402 The Hubble Space Telescope has photographed all the planets of our Solar System except two: Earth and Mercury. The telescope is too close to the Earth, so it is not possible to take a clear picture of the planet. Mercury, on the other hand, is too close to the Sun, and the planet's intense reflected light could damage the telescope.

Satellites

403 There are two kinds of satellites: first are the heavenly bodies, that are also called moons of a planet, and second, man-made satellites that are placed into space by humans. Earth has only one natural satellite, which is the moon that we see in the sky. However, we now have thousands of man-made satellites that are continuously revolving around the Earth.

404 Apart from the thousands of artificial satellites already launched into outer space by humans, more than 100 new satellites are launched into space each year. Several of those satellites are space telescopes that are helpful for the observation and research on weather around the Earth.

405 Each satellite has its own orbit on which it revolves. A satellite with a low orbit must fly faster in order to avoid falling back to the Earth. Most artificial or man-made satellites fly in low orbits at approximately 300 kilometres from the surface of the Earth.

406 Most of the planets have their own natural satellites which are known as moons. There are also planets that have no moons. However, did you know, there are also some moons that have their own moons? Three of such moons are Saturn's moon Titan, Jupiter's moon Lo, and Neptune's moon Triton.

SATELLITES

407 **Our Solar System has eight planets and each planet is different in size.** Similarly, the natural satellites of the planets also vary in size. Jupiter is the largest planet in our Solar System and coincidently its moon Ganymede is the largest moon among all the other moons in the Solar System.

408 **Saturn's moon Titan is different from many other moons because, firstly, it has its own moon, and secondly, it has a significant atmosphere.** None of the other moons in the Solar System have such a dense atmosphere. In fact, its atmosphere is denser than any of the other terrestrial planets except for Venus.

409 **The Moon's orbit around the Earth is elliptical and that is why once in a while the Moon comes very close to the Earth.** This occurrence is referred to as the Supermoon. During this time, the Moon looks larger than usual. The last Supermoon was seen on November 14, 2016 and the next Supermoon will take place on November 25, 2034.

ASTRONOMY

410 **Sputnik 1 was the world's first ever artificial satellite that was sent into the space.** It was launched on October 4, 1957 by the then Soviet Union. The launch of this satellite inaugurated the space age. It was a capsule that weighed 83.6 kilograms. It remained in the Earth's orbit until early 1958, after which it fell back towards the Earth, burning in the atmosphere as it entered the atmosphere.

411 **On November 3, 1957, Soviet Union launched Sputnik 2, the first satellite to carry a living animal in it.** A dog named Laika was placed inside a cabin with a temperature control system. After this, eight more Sputnik missions were carried out which launched similar satellites with various animals on board to test the spacecraft's life-support systems.

412 Only three months after the launch of the first artificial satellite by the Soviet Union, the USA launched their first artificial satellite, Explorer 1, into space orbit on January 31, 1958. It was launched as part of the US contribution to in the International Geophysical Year. The launch of this satellite also marked the beginning of the space race between the USA and Soviet Union.

SATELLITES

413 An artificial satellite has two important components, firstly, an antenna to receive and send information, and secondly, a power source that could be a battery or a solar panel. To stay in space, a satellite must travel at a speed that is called its orbital velocity. The orbital velocity of a satellite needs to be approximately more than 28,200 kilometres per hour.

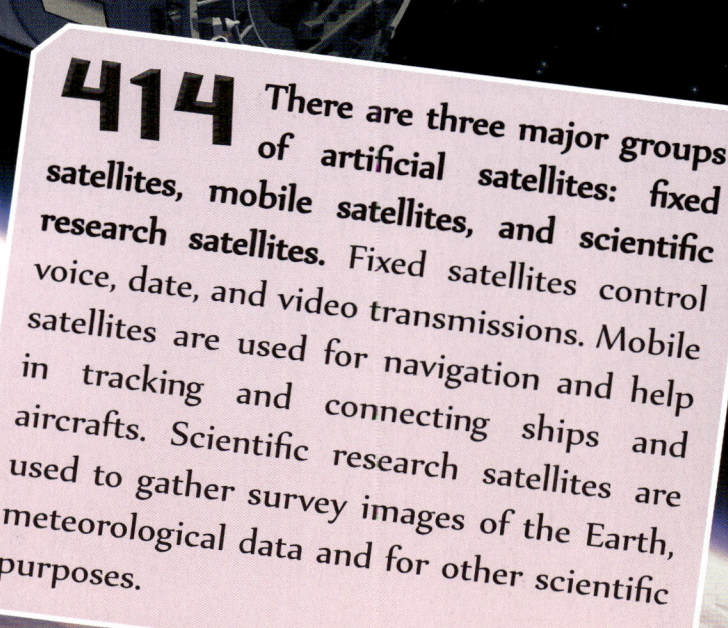

414 There are three major groups of artificial satellites: fixed satellites, mobile satellites, and scientific research satellites. Fixed satellites control voice, date, and video transmissions. Mobile satellites are used for navigation and help in tracking and connecting ships and aircrafts. Scientific research satellites are used to gather survey images of the Earth, meteorological data and for other scientific purposes.

Rockets

415 Did you know the earliest rockets were made by the Chinese in the 13th century? The Song dynasty of China contributed to several technological advances in history. During a war in the late 13th century, they employed the earliest known gunpowder-propelled rockets. The earliest form of those rockets was the archaic fire arrow.

416 The Chinese experimented with makeshift rockets at first to create noise and explosions for festivals, but later these rockets evolved into weapons during the Ki-Keng war with the Mongols. These were not like our modern rockets with engines inside them; instead, they were made of bamboo tubes filled with gunpowder made from charcoal dust, sulphur, and saltpetre.

417 The Mongols started copying the Chinese rockets. They are believed to have spread the use of rockets across Europe. However, these were still very different from the rockets that we use to go into outer space today.

418 The first-ever rocket that crossed the boundary of space was the German V2. It was a ballistic missile used by the Nazis during World War II. It was quite powerful, and went up 100 kilometres from the surface of the Earth.

ROCKETS

419 Wernher von Braun was an aerospace engineer and space architect who had designed the V2 rocket that was launched in 1942. Wernher von Braun started working with NASA in the United States after the war. He worked at NASA during the infancy of the organisation. He was also the chief architect of the superbooster, Saturn V. This was the rocket that propelled the Apollo missions to the moon.

420 Robert Hutchings Goddard is considered to be the father of modern rocketry. He is also considered to be the man who ushered in the Space Age. In 1926, Goddard made the first liquid-fuelled rocket. He has 214 patented inventions but two of them stand out as important milestones towards spaceflight; one of them was a multi-stage rocket, and the other was the liquid-fuelled rocket.

421 It was on March 26, 1926 that Robert Goddard built and tested the first liquid-fuelled rocket. The rocket was fuelled by liquid oxygen and gasoline. The rocket climbed up towards the sky for 12.5 metres before landing in a nearby cabbage patch. It had climbed 12 metres in only 2.5 seconds.

ASTRONOMY

422 **More than a million pounds of thrust is produced once a typical rocket launches.** A rocket can travel at the speed of 35,000 kilometres per hour and can easily carry 2,700 kilograms of weight inside it. In its first moments after the lift-off, the heat produced by a rocket could heat 85,000 homes for a full day.

423 **There is a family of American missiles and space launch vehicles by the name of Atlas.** The original Atlas missile was initially designed in the late 1950s. Many years later, in 2006, the active expendable launch system, Atlas V was developed, which set a record for being the fastest rocket. Its travelling speed in the atmosphere was around 58,000 kilometres per hour and it topped out at around 75,000 kilometres per hour.

424 **The R-7ICBM was the first rocket that launched an artificial satellite into the orbit of the Earth.** It was designed by the Soviet Union, and was modified to launch Sputnik 1 into space.

ROCKETS

425 SpaceX, a company pioneering commercial space travel, was the first to launch a private satellite to orbit the Earth. Falcon 9 was an unmanned capsule launched on December 10, 2010 by the company. It orbited the Earth two times before landing into the Pacific.

426 Although Yuri Gagarin was the first man to travel into space in a rocket, orbiting the Earth once on April 12, 1961, it was Apollo 11 that made the first-ever Moon landing on July 20, 1969. The first two men who walked on the Moon were Neil Armstrong and Buzz Aldrin. The command module was manned by Michael Collins.

427 When rocket boosters return to the Earth, they fall into the ocean. These rocket boosters are made in a way that they can be reused once they fall into the water. However, they usually require a lot of repair due to the damage that is caused by the salt water of the ocean, and the pressure they face in passing through the Earth's atmosphere.

ASTRONOMY

428 **Many companies are working to make rockets that can be used multiple times without requiring extensive repair.** This would help make space travel much easier. The company, SpaceX, have even managed to land an unmanned rocket on a launch pad on land. They are trying to do a similar landing on a pad at sea.

429 **The launch pad is the largest vehicle ever constructed.** It carries rockets to their launch sites. It takes around half an hour to travel 1,800 feet. Rockets also use immensely large parachutes to slow down their descent when they return to Earth. Some of these parachutes are hundreds of feet wide.

430 **The solid rocket motor is the largest solid propellant motor ever developed for spaceflight.** It was first built to be used on a manned spacecraft. The motor was composed of an ignition system, a segmented motor case that was loaded with solid propellants (instead of liquid fuel), a nozzle that was moveable, and some other necessary hardware.

431

More than one million pounds of propellant is used in each solid rocket motor. At a testing plant in Utah, America, a company in association with NASA has been testing and improving the solid rocket motor. Here, three different mixer buildings were located to mix the propellant in 600-gallon bowls. Only then was the propellant taken to special casting buildings where it was poured into the casting segments.

432

The Royal Institute of Technology (KTH) in Sweden has discovered a new molecule that may be an important component of rocket fuel in future. The name of that new molecule is 'Trinitramide'. This fuel is said to be more than 20 per cent effective in comparison to the best rocket fuels we have at present.

433

Orion is a spacecraft built by NASA to take humans farther into space than they have ever gone before. It will mainly serve as the exploration vehicle that will carry the crew to space, sustain the crew during the space travel, provide emergency abort capability, and also provide safe re-entry from deep space return velocities. NASA's new heavy-lift rocket, the Space Launch System (SLS), will launch Orion.

ASTRONOMY

434 **The Space Launch System is a new mega rocket by NASA.** It is a towering booster especially designed for deep space missions. The SLS will be ready for its first test flight no later than November 2018. It will be the largest rocket ever constructed and will take humans farther into space than before. This launcher could take the NASA astronauts to an asteroid or even to Mars sometime in the future.

435 **A Rhesus monkey, Albert II, was the first mammal in space.** A previous mission carrying another monkey, Albert I, had been unsuccessful but on June 14, 1949, the second Albert reached a distance of 83 miles. He was anaesthetised during the flight. Sensors were also implanted to check on his vital signs but unfortunately, he died upon impact while re-entering the Earth's atmosphere.

436 **The United States was experimenting with monkeys, but the Soviet Union was experimenting with sending dogs into space.** The Soviet Union had slots for almost 57 dogs who would go into space during the 1950s and 60s. In reality, some of the animals went on more than one flight.

437 **The Soviet Union R-1 111A-1 launched the first dogs, Tsygan and Dezik, into space.** On July 22, 1951, the dogs reached space, but they did not orbit the Earth. The mission was successful as these dogs were the first mammals that were recovered alive after a spaceflight. Two dogs, Belka and Strelka, were then sent into space after Laika on August 19, 1960. They were the first animals to orbit the Earth and return alive.

438 **A chimpanzee called Ham, named after the Holloman Aerospace Medical Centre, was trained to perform tasks during a spaceflight.** His flight took place on January 31, 1961, and he became a popular celebrity afterwards! The chimpanzee learned to pull levers to receive banana pellets and avoid electric shocks. He was the first animal to not only ride in a space vessel, but also interact with it.

Humans in Space

439 On April 12, 1961, the Soviet Union launched the first human spaceflight. It was a part of the Vostok programme. Yuri Gagarin was the first Cosmonaut, and marked the start of the human presence in space. Today, humans are constantly pushing back the boundaries of how far they can go into outer space. In fact, for over 16 years now, humans have been continually present in space, on the International Space Station.

440 The Mercury programmes were the early efforts made by the United States to launch a human spaceflight. Alan Shepard, an American astronaut, went into space on May 1961, for a brief time, but did not orbit the Earth. He was sent on the Mercury 3 mission.

441 On May 5, 1961, Alan Shepard made the first US piloted spaceflight in the Mercury Freedom 7. Shepard reached an altitude of 186 kilometres during the suborbital mission that lasted 15 minutes and 22 seconds. The Mercury spacecraft along with the astronaut were recovered by the USS Champlain 483 kilometres downrange from Cape Canaveral in the Atlantic Ocean.

442 **The Mercury programme had several spectacular successes.** For instance, in February 1962, the astronaut John Glenn, who was a naval officer and an aviator, spent five hours in orbit on the mission of Mercury 6.

443 **In June 1965, the US astronaut Edward White became the first American to 'walk' in space.** He was the pilot of the Gemini-Titan IV space flight, and made his spacewalk from this craft.

444 On June 3, 1965, Edward White performed an Extra Vehicular Activity (**EVA or spacewalk**). It was the third revolution of the Gemini IV spacecraft when he floated into zero gravity. For this flight, he was awarded the NASA Distinguished Service Medal and was also awarded the Congressional Space Medal of Honour posthumously.

445 **The Gemini was an enlarged spacecraft introduced by NASA after Mercury.** It was a redesigned spacecraft meant for two astronauts. Gemini missions were manned by a crew of 10 from 1964 to 1966. Their mission was to improve techniques of spacecraft control and extravehicular activity, that is, spacewalking.

ASTRONOMY

446 **The very first time in history two vehicles manoeuvred to meet in space was on December 15, 1965.** On that day, Gemini 6, which was piloted by Wally Schirra and Tom Stafford, pulled within 1 foot of Gemini 7, which was piloted by Frank Borman and Jim Lovell.

447 **A photograph of the Gemini 7 spacecraft was taken from the hatch window of the Gemini 6 spacecraft.** The picture was taken during the rendezvous and station-keeping manoeuvres on December 15, 1965. The space crafts were about nine feet apart, at an altitude of approximately 258 kilometres.

448 **On February 20, 1962, John Herschel Glenn Jr. became the first American to orbit the Earth.** He flew the Friendship 7 mission that was launched on a Mercury-Atlas rocket. In 1959, NASA selected the 'Mercury Seven' group of military test pilots to fly the Project Mercury spacecraft, and Glenn was one of these men, who went on to become America's first astronauts.

HUMANS IN SPACE

449 **The USSR launched five cosmonauts in the Vostok capsules.** On June 16, 1963, Valentina Vladimirovna Tereshkova became the first woman to fly into outer space aboard Vostok 6. She was selected from more than four hundred applicants and five finalists to pilot the space vessel. In her three days in space, she completed 48 orbits of our planet.

450 **In 1964 and 1965, the Soviet Union launched two orbital flights.** In March 1965, Voskhod 2 went into space on a manned mission. Alexey Leonov became the first Russian to leave the spacecraft and perform a twelve-minute spacewalk. It was another milestone in space exploration.

451

The Saturn-V rocket was developed by the United States to send the Apollo spacecraft to the Moon. In December 1968, Frank Borman, James Lovell, and William Anders were launched in Apollo 8 shuttle by the Saturn-V rocket. They orbited the Moon 10 times.

ASTRONOMY

452 **The Apollo 11 spaceship landed on the Moon in July 1969.** Neil Armstrong and Buzz Aldrin were the first humans to walk on the moon. They landed on the Moon on July 21 and returned safely on July 24.

453 **By 1972, 12 men had landed on the Moon via six different Apollo missions.** Half of them drove electric-powered vehicles on the surface of the Moon. However, Apollo 13 could not land on the Moon, as it experienced a catastrophic in-flight failure. The crew members included Lovell, Jack Swigert, and Fred Haise. All of them returned to Earth safely.

454 **The Shenzhou spacecraft was designed by China, and it resembled the Russian Soyuz spaceships.** China became the third nation to achieve independent human spacecraft capability when it launched Yang Liwei on October 15, 2003, on a 21-hour flight aboard Shenzhou 5.

HUMANS IN SPACE

455 Several private spaceflight ventures have been undertaken since the early 2000s. Many companies have been planning for advanced human spaceflight. Some of these companies are Blue Origin, SpaceX, Virgin Galactic, and Sierra Nevada. All these four companies are developing programmes to fly commercial passengers into outer space.

456 In September 2011, China launched the Tiangong-1 space station and two sortie missions to it. The first was Shenzhou 9, from June 16 to 29 2012, which had China's first female astronaut Liu Yang. The second was Shenzhou 10, from June 13 to 26, 2013. However, the Chinese Space station was retired on March 21, 2016.

457 Spaceship Two has been developed by Virgin Galactic, and is a commercial suborbital spacecraft aimed at the space tourism market. It is believed that it might be ready for regular space flights by the year 2018. A multi-year test programme by the company Blue Origin has already carried out six successful unmanned test flights in their New Shepard vehicle in 2015–2016. They too are planning to initiate commercial flights in 2018.

458 The first woman to walk in space was Svetlana Savitskaya. She undertook this spacewalk on July 25, 1984. Just a year earlier, in 1983, Sally Ride became the first American woman in space. In 1999, with shuttle mission STS-93, Eileen Collins became the first American female space shuttle pilot.

459 Valeri Polyakov left Earth on January 8, 1994, and did not return until March 22, 1995. This was the longest single human spaceflight, with a total of 437 days 17 hours 58 minutes and 16 seconds. However, it was Sergei Krikalev who spent the longest time in space, which was 803 days 9 hours and 39 minutes altogether, adding the time of his various spaceflights.

460 For many years, only the Soviet Union (present day Russia) and the United States had their own astronauts. The flight of Vladimir Remek, a Czech, initiated the flight of the citizens from other nations into the space. He flew on a Soviet spacecraft in the Interkosmos programme on March 2, 1978. Till 2010, citizens from 38 nations have been to space in Soviet, American, Russian, and Chinese spacecraft.

Space Probes

461 **Small space crafts are often sent to the space for measuring distances between planets and other heavenly bodies.** These are known as space probes. When they travel to distant planets, space probes try to save fuel by using the other planet's gravity to catapult them on their way. This is known as a slingshot.

462 **In the year 1959, Luna 3 was launched by the Soviet Union.** It was the first mission to photograph the far side of the Moon. Later on, in January 1966, Luna 9 was launched, which was the first man-made object to soft land on the surface of the Moon, or for that matter, on any extra-terrestrial surface.

463 **The Soviet Luna programme launched Luna 16 on September 12, 1970, which was an unmanned space mission.** It was the first robotic space probe from Earth to the Moon that returned with a sample of lunar soil after five unsuccessful attempts.

ASTRONOMY

464 **Mariner 9 was part of the Mariner programme launched by NASA.** It was an unmanned space probe that was launched on May 30, 1971. It greatly contributed to the exploration of Mars. It reached the planet on November 14, 1971.

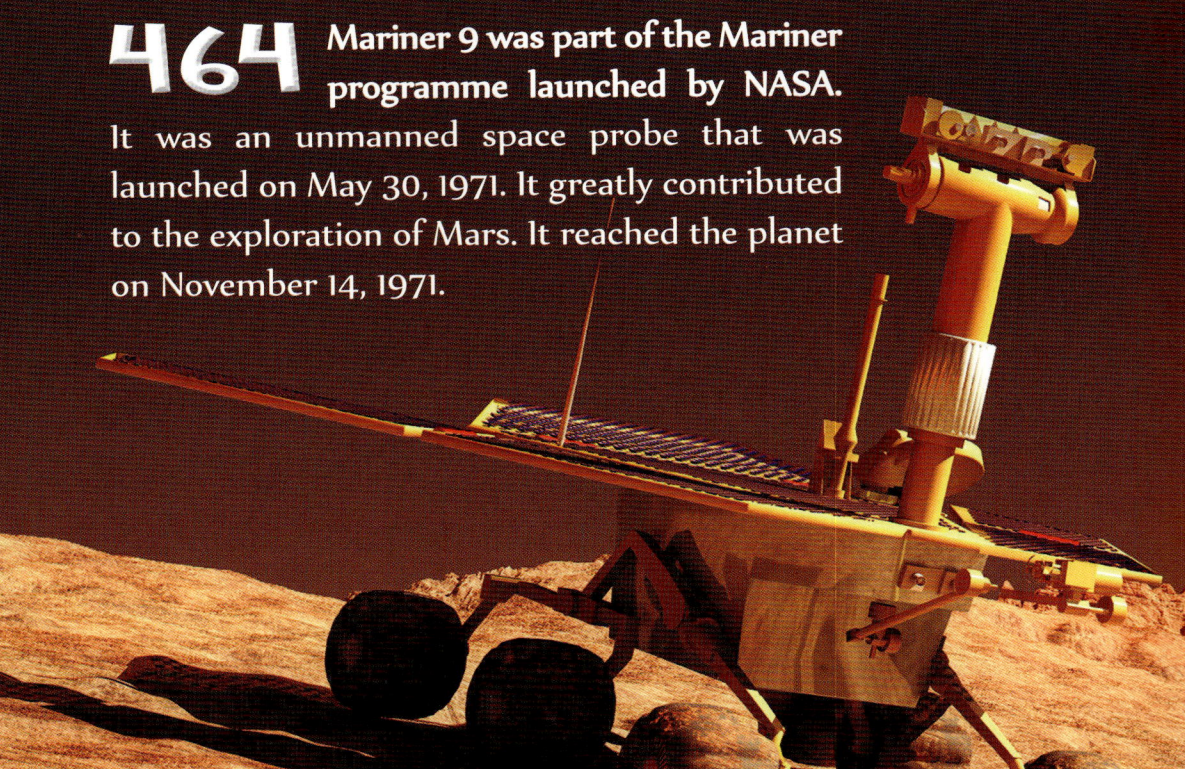

465 **On November 3, 1973, NASA launched Mariner 10 as a robotic space probe.** It was launched two years after Mariner 9 and was the last in the Mariner programme. It was sent to fly past the planets Mercury and Venus. Mariner 10 was the first space probe to Mercury.

466 **The Soviet Union launched the Lunokhod programme in 1970.** Lunokhod 1 was the first of two unmanned lunar rovers that were landed on the Moon by the USSR. It was carried by the Luna 17 spacecraft to the Moon on November 10, 1970. It was the first remote-controlled robot that freely moved on an astronomical object besides the Earth.

SPACE PROBES

467 **The Soviet Venera programme was launched for the exploration of the planet Venus.** As part of this programme, Venera 4 was launched on June 12, 1967. It is said to be the first successful programme to analyse the environment of another planet in our Solar System.

468 Venera 7 was another space probe that was a part of the Venera series of probes to the planet **Venus.** It was the first space probe to have a soft landing on another planet and then transmit the data from there to the Earth.

469 **The Soviet Union operated another space programme between 1960 and 1973.** Mars 3 was an unmanned probe that was launched on May 28, 1971. It achieved the first soft landing on the planet Mars but shortly after its landing, the spacecraft failed.

ASTRONOMY

470 **The first successful rover on the planet Mars was Sojourner.** It was operated by NASA from the United States. It landed on the planet on July 4, 1997, and explored Mars for approximately three months. The rover was equipped with front and rear cameras along with hardware that could conduct several scientific experiments.

471 **Space probes have been used to examine comets as well.** One of these was Halley Armada that was sent to observe the Halley's Comet during its journey in 1985–86 through the inner Solar System. One of these probes was operated by the European Space Agency, two of them were joint projects of the Soviet Union and France, while the other two projects were operated by the Institute of Space and Astronautical Science of Japan, which is now integrated with National Space Development Agency of Japan (NASDA) to form Japan Aerospace Exploration Agency (JAXA).

472 **The Mars Exploration Rovers is an ongoing mission by NASA that involves two robotic space rovers, Spirit and Opportunity.** Both of them were launched in 2003 and reached the planet in 2004. They were sent to search for clues related to the presence of water on the planet and also to study the surface and geology of the planet.

SPACE PROBES

473 **On March 22, 2010, communication with the Mars rover Spirit stopped.** Continuous attempts were made to regain contact with the rover but finally, on March 24, 2011, NASA announced that the efforts to contact and communicate with the unresponsive rover had finally ended.

474 **The robotic rovers Spirit and Opportunity were landed on two different sides of the planet Mars.** While Spirit had ceased communicating, Opportunity is still actively working as of 2016. The rovers lasted for more than twelve years on Mars, whereas they were intended to last only three months.

475 **The International Cometary Explorer (ICE) was originally a solar observatory that was sent into solar orbit in 1985 to make the first observation of Comet Giacobini-Zinner.** It was the first spacecraft to visit a comet. It was operated by NASA as a prelude to studies on Halley's Comet.

476 On February 7, 1999, a robotic space probe, Stardust, was launched by NASA. Its primary mission was to collect samples from the comets and the cosmic dust before returning to Earth for analysis. It was the first time that such a sample-return mission took place.

477 The first space probe to land on an asteroid was the Near Earth Asteroid Rendezvous–Shoemaker, popularly known as the NEAR–Shoemaker. It was named after the planetary scientist Eugene Shoemaker and was launched on February 17, 1996. It orbited the near-Earth asteroid Eros several times and finally was terminated after it touched down on the asteroid on February 12, 2001.

478 The first asteroid sample-return mission was Hayabusa 2. It was launched on December 3, 2014, and was operated by the Japanese space agency JAXA. It followed on from the previous space probe Hayabusa that was launched on May 9, 2003, and addressed the weak points that were learned from that mission.

SPACE PROBES

479 A US space probe, Pioneer 10, was the first mission to the planet Jupiter. The space probe was launched on March 2, 1972, and it was the first spacecraft to traverse the asteroid belt. About 500 images were transmitted from Jupiter but the radio communications were lost from the spacecraft on January 23, 2003.

480 NASA has operated a space probe by the name of Dawn. It was launched on September 27, 2007, and its mission was to study two of the three known proto-planets of the asteroid belt, Vesta and Ceres. It is the first space probe to visit a dwarf planet.

Space Stations

481 **The International Space Station (ISS) is a habitable, man-made satellite.** It has pressurised modules that are fit for the astronauts to live inside. The ISS orbits the Earth at an altitude of between 330 km and 435 km. In 1998, its first component was launched into space and now it is the largest artificial body in the Earth's orbit. It can also be seen with the naked eye from the Earth's surface.

482 **The US had started the project of building a space station which was delayed due to funding and technical issues.** Originally it was called 'Freedom' in the 1980s by the then US President Ronald Reagan. It was in 1993 that the USA and Russia merged their separate space station plans incorporating contributions from the European Space Agency (ESA) and Japan. It then came to be known as the ISS.

483 **The first space station of the United States was Skylab.** It was launched and operated by NASA. It spent six years orbiting the Earth from 1973 to 1979, after which it fell back to the Earth.

484 **Three manned missions were made to Skylab, which were SL-2, SL-3, and SL-4.** Of these, SL-2 was launched on 25 May 1973, and was its first manned mission. The crew inside the Skylab stayed in orbit for 28 days. The next mission was launched on July 28, 1973, and the crew remained in orbit for 59 days. The last mission was launched on November 16, 1973, where the crew spent 84 days in orbit. SL-4 returned to Earth on February 8, 1974.

485 **A module called Zarya was the first part of the International Space Station that was sent into space.** On November 20, 1998, the module was launched on a Russian Proton rocket and sent to space. After two weeks, NASA attached another module called Unity aboard the Space Shuttle Endeavour to the Zarya module. This new module contained all the requirements that were used for long term human living in space.

ASTRONOMY

486 The ISS is 357 feet in length, which means the space station's total area is the size of an American football field. It is the largest artificial body in space orbit. It includes more than six bedrooms, two bathrooms, and a gymnasium. The weight of the ISS is nearly 419,500 kilograms. It is four times bigger than Mir, the Russian space station, and five times larger than Skylab, the United States space station.

487 On October 31, 2000, the first ISS crew mission was launched on the Russian spacecraft Soyuz, called 'Expedition 1'. On November 2, 2000, three Russian cosmonauts docked and entered the ISS. Since then, the space station has been continuously occupied, marking the longest continuous human presence in space orbit.

488 As of 2013, astronauts and cosmonauts from 15 different nations have visited the ISS. A total of 352 flights have been made to the ISS by 211 people. Out of these people, 31 were women and seven were 'space tourists'. In addition, 76 people have made a trip to the ISS twice and 25 people have made a trip thrice, while five people have been to the station four times.

489 The project of developing the ISS was a joint venture involving five major space agencies, including NASA of the United States, Roskosmos of Russia, CSA of Canada, JAXA of Japan, and the ESA, which is made up of agencies from Brazil, France, Italy, Malaysia, and South Korea.

ASTRONOMY

490 An expedition to the ISS can last up to six months. As of 2013, there had been 38 such expeditions to the space station. Earlier these expeditions had a crew of three members, which was later reduced to two people due to safety concerns. In one day, the ISS completes 15.5 orbits. This means that crew members experience a sunrise or sunset every 92 minutes!

491 The ISS also helped a lot in ending the space race between nations and spreading an international understanding of knowledge related to space. According to the US agency NASA, "the ISS has more than 100,000 people working for space agencies and more than 500 contractor facilities in 37 US states and 16 countries." Sixty-eight countries have been involved on the research regarding the ISS.

SPACE STATIONS

492 The US comedian Stephan Colbert once won a NASA competition held in 2009. The winner was supposed to have a module of ISS named after them. However, NASA finally decided to name the module 'Tranquillity' instead. They ultimately named a treadmill after the American comedian and called it the Combined Operational Load Bearing External Resistance Treadmill (C.O.L.B.E.R.T.).

493 In a space station, it is important for an astronaut to have a good airflow around them while they sleep. Otherwise they could wake up gasping for oxygen, because around their heads, a bubble of their own exhaled carbon dioxide would form.

494 There is no gravity in space and hence, a space station is also deprived of the gravitational force that we would experience on Earth. This condition makes it impossible for an astronaut to cry, because the weightless environment prevent tears from falling down—instead they collect in little balls and sting the eyes.

ASTRONOMY

495 In a space station, an astronaut cannot taste food the way they can taste it when on the ground. The reason is the loss of gravity, which makes it difficult for the food to go down the throat of an astronaut. Instead, the astronaut's sinuses can get clogged up. This makes the food tasteless.

496 A space suit comprises of different kinds of equipment especially designed for the well-being of a person who has to live in a zero-gravity environment. There is even a velcro patch inside the helmet of the suit so that the astronauts can scratch their nose whenever they need!

SPACE STATIONS

497 Voting is one of the rights of a citizen of any country. Therefore, the American astronauts that live in the International Space Station have the liberty to take part in their national elections by voting from space, though a secure.

498 There is a lack of oxygen in outer space and it is very difficult for the astronauts to breathe. To overcome the situation, there are 'oxygen candles' that are especially used on the International Space Station. When these candles are ignited, enough oxygen is produced for one person to breathe for 24 hours.

ASTRONOMY

499 The space station Mir operated in a low orbit of Earth from 1986 to 2001. It was run by the Soviet Union and later on by Russia. It was the first modular space station that was assembled in orbit, from 1986 to 1996. The mass of Mir was greater than any other previous space stations.

500 Mir holds the record for the longest single human spaceflight, when Valeri Polyakov spent 437 days and 18 hours on it between 1994 and 1995. Out of its 15-year lifespan, Mir was occupied for a total of 12-and-a-half-years. It had the capacity to support a resident crew of three members or even more, for short visits.